Ghost Railways of Ontario

Ghost Railways of Ontario

Ron Brown

Polar Bear Press, Toronto

distributed by:
North 49 Books
35 Prince Andrew Place
Toronto, Ontario M3C 2H2
416 449-4000
north49@idirect.com

Canadian Cataloguing in Publication Data

Brown, Ron, 1945-
 Ghost railways of Ontario

includes bibliographical references and index.
ISBN 1-896757-05-7

1. Railroads – Ontario – Guidebooks   2. Ontario – Guidebooks.   I. Title

HE2809.05B76 1998   385.09713   C98-930676-3

Printed in Canada

10 9 8 7 6 5 4 3

Contents

Introduction

Ignore for a moment urban Ontario's appearance, its sprawling suburbs and congested highways – Ontario's cities, towns, and villages are the creation of the railway age. From that June day in 1853, when Ontario's first steam engine puffed north from Toronto to Machel's Corners (today's Aurora), the locations of railways and their stations would shape the landscape and the destiny of urban Ontario.

If the steel rails came to a fledgling pioneer town, the place boomed and prospered; if they went elsewhere, the town dwindled, perhaps dying and becoming a ghost town.

It was little wonder, then, that the local politicians of the mid 1800s lobbied hard for railways. Many communities scrimped on necessary expenses, such as for roads, to lure a railway company.

The next three decades marked a spate of railway promotion, building, and sometimes just wishful thinking. While early trunk lines, like the Great Western and the Canada Southern, were just short cuts across Ontario for American lines, the Grand Trunk, built from Montreal to Sarnia, would be Ontario's first main railway artery. From it hopeful promoters built dozens of smaller lines into the hinterland to bring lumber, freight, and passengers to the main trunk line.

By the 1880s the dreams of the small railway promoters were in tatters, the revenue less than hoped. Many of the small lines were grabbed up by the Grand Trunk, while the fledgling CPR began to amass their Ontario network by absorbing others. When, around the turn of the century, the ambitious Canadian Northern Railway project of MacKenzie and Mann resulted in a third main line from Toronto eastward, Ontario became the domain of just 3 main railway companies.

During these formative years, the railways were shaping Ontario's landscape. Where the railways were built through existing communities, the presence of a station brought with it the usual coal dock and water tank, but also businesses like feed mills, hotels, even YMCA's, and here and there a brothel.

Where towns hadn't existed previously, the railways simply built one. Here they would design a main street that ended at the station door, while a grid network of streets accommodated workers' homes. Where a town stood nearby, a satellite village would cluster around the station, consisting of a hotel, store and a handful of houses.

World War One brought a sudden change in the fortunes of Canada's railways, bankrupting both the Grand Trunk and the

Canadian Northern. As a result, the Canadian National Railway was created by the government of Canada to take over the bankrupt lines and turn around their fortunes. One way to start was to eliminate redundant lines, and so Ontario's first ghost railways began to appear. One of the first was MacKenzie and Mann's Canadian Northern line between Toronto and Ottawa. By the 1940s only the section between Napanee and Ottawa remained.

Competition from cars and trucks sank many of the slower branch lines and the 1950s saw the beginning of the end for Ontario's branch line railways. Dozens were abandoned, a trend that has accelerated right into the 1990s. Despite the clogged roads and the polluted air from the excessive road traffic that has resulted, there seems no intent to reverse the decline in rail lines.

Trunk lines like the Canadian Northern, pioneer lines like the Hamilton and Northwestern and the Cobourg and Peterborough, resource lines like the Kingston and Pembroke, and the Central Ontario, portage lines that linked the lakes, like the Midland, and the Stratford and Port Dover - all of them are now silent, the rattle of the boxcars and the shriek of the steam stilled forever.

These are the ghost railways of Ontario.

Most have left an indelible legacy on the landscape. Rights of way, now silent, yet pass the stations, the hotels, and the feed mills, or ford the rivers on bridgeless abutments; main streets end at a strange open space where the station once stood; and in the ghost towns, empty windows, like sad eyes, gaze back upon an era that will never be repeated. It is a legacy that is vanishing. Stations and hotels are being burned down or demolished, and rights of way are being developed over, or ploughed under.

History lovers have struggled to reverse the decimation. In some cases they have succeeded. In 1989 the government of Canada, stung by the clandestine razing of the magnificent West Toronto station by a callous CPR, passed legislation designed specifically to save stations. Since then, more than 100 have been rescued from oblivion. Trail groups have saved many miles of ghost railways for snowmobilers, joggers, cyclists and equestrians, happy to be free of the anxiety of traffic and photo radar.

This book is your guide to this legacy. It divides the province into four regions, and leads you along the old lines, using the names under which they first enjoyed prominence. Although the directions are for car travel, you can nonetheless follow the route of the early engineers and pass through the towns and the landscapes that they did.

Along some you will find ghost towns, railway stations, and old bridges, along others the industries and townscapes that the railways created. Along some you can follow the right of way itself.

Here are a few useful tips to remember:

- Although this book offers sketch maps, the maps you should have with you are the Ontario Ministry of Transportation 1:250,000 series road maps. These maps show you all roads and most of their numbers, as well as all towns and villages, and even the place names of communities that have long vanished.

- Respect private property. It takes only one bad experience for an owner to deny to others the heritage they own. Get permission before taking pictures from on a private property (you are legally allowed to photograph anything from a public vantage.) Once there you will find that most owners enjoy talking about their heritage.

- When following rights of way, use safety sense. Don't try driving over old railway bridges that might not have been maintained for a number of years. Unmaintained rights of way could suffer from windfalls or washouts, or be under spring high water. Check ahead first.

But above all, cherish this vanishing railway heritage while you can. Much of what you see today may be gone tomorrow.

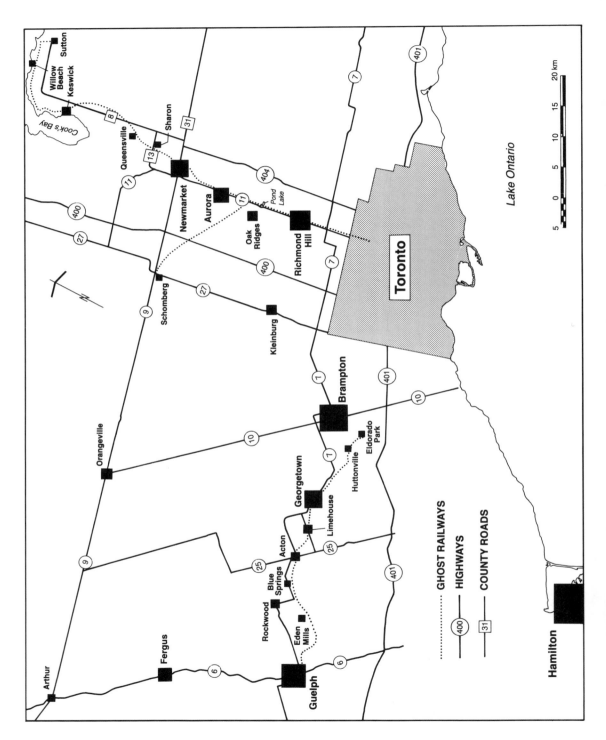

CHAPTER ONE:

Before "GO":
The Toronto Area's First Commuter Railways

Backgrounder

The year was 1890. Toronto was booming. Union Station was over capacity, the shoreline in front of it vanishing beneath slimy landfill and rail yards which sent a pall of coal smoke over the downtown.

Meanwhile, in the purer air of Toronto's suburbs a land boom was under way. In this heady period a group of business men decided to build a new railway line. Radical in approach, it would encircle the booming city and would link the radial railway lines then being extended outward to Toronto's hinterlands.

This was to be the Belt Line Railway.

It would consist of two belts. Starting from a station in the Don Valley, the Rosedale station, one loop would creep up the valley from the Don River towards Mount Pleasant Cemetery. Then it would angle northwest to Bathurst Street and then bend west to the Grand Trunk Line and follow it south into the city. From Davenport station, located immediately south of St. Clair, a second loop would venture westerly to

Lambton and follow a route southerly along the east bank of the Humber River to Swansea Station on the western branch of the Grand Trunk Railway line.

The plan called for ten stations, two of which it would share with the Grand Trunk, those at Davenport and Parkdale. While most of the other stations were flag stations, the one at Moore Park was the pride of the line. Of all the new suburbs that the Belt Line served, Moore Park would be the wealthiest. To fit in with the palatial homes and wide lawns, local architect John Moore designed a grand station. With its four turrets, the station would be the centre piece of a large park where Moore envisioned flower beds, and arbours with walkways and seats for the area inhabitants.

But Moore's park was never built. After two years the boom collapsed and the Belt Line's short life was over. The route was absorbed by the Grand Trunk and used only as an industrial spur.

The suburban radial lines, however, were much more successful. It had begun as the Metropolitan Railway, and the radial line's first cars were pulled by horses along Yonge Street between Summerhill and Eglinton. In 1890 the plodding horses were replaced by speedier electrical streetcars. Following the demise of the Belt Line, the suburban growth recovered and beckoned the radial line northward; it had reached Glen Echo by 1892 and Newmarket by 1899. And to attract even more customers, the radial line entered the commercial recreation business. In 1899 it opened a 200-acre park around the shores of Bond Lake, a small post-glacial pond on Yonge Street on the southern fringe of the community of Oak Ridges.

Radial fever was in full swing and radial lines were built westward to Port Credit in 1905 and eastward to West Hill in 1906. Like the Metropolitan, the Toronto and Scarborough Railway built parks to gain more revenue. Victoria Park at the foot of Blantyre, the Toronto Hunt Club on Kingston Road at Warden, and Scarborough Heights Park, east of St. Clair and also on Kingston Road, were all electrical railway parks.

But up to this point the lines all followed roads: the Metropolitan followed Yonge Street; the Scarborough, Kingston Road; and the Mimico, Lakeshore Blvd.

Enter William MacKenzie, of Canadian Northern fame. In 1904 MacKenzie, who along with Donald Mann was building a railway empire from coast to coast, bought up most of the radials and began building across the countryside. The Toronto and York, an extension of the Metropolitan, was completed into Sutton on Lake Simcoe in 1909 while a branch line to Schomberg, known as the Schomberg and Aurora

branch, had been added in 1904. In 1911 Mackenzie added the Toronto Suburban, then a small streetcar line in west-end Toronto, and by 1917 had extended the line from Weston to Guelph with twenty station stops along the way.

In 1912 when Adam Beck and Ontario Hydro entered the fray, electric lines were suddenly everywhere: from Kitchener through Galt and Brantford to Port Dover on Lake Erie, from London to Port Stanley, from Brantford to Hamilton, from Hamilton to Beamsville and from Port Dalhousie to Port Colborne.

In 1922, with Mackenzie and his Canadian Northern bankrupt, Toronto's newly formed Toronto Transit Commission took over the radials within the city, while Ontario Hydro took over the Toronto and York to Sutton. Meanwhile, the Canadian National Railway had been formed to take over Canada's many bankrupt lines and ended up with MacKenzie's myriad electric lines across the province. The CNR even resumed construction of the Toronto Eastern, a line projected form the Belt Line to Cobourg that was abandoned in 1913. Similarly the CNR failed to finish it. Then, reminiscent of the Metropolitan's practice, the CNR purchased Eldorado Park, a pleasant retreat in the valley of the Credit River west of Brampton, to lure more passengers.

But the growth of the auto era meant the end of the radials. In 1927 the Schomberg branch was the first to go, followed in 1931 by the Toronto Suburban to Guelph. By 1936 most lines were abandoned, the last to go being the old Metropolitan line to Richmond Hill in 1948.

During the 1930s, to add to the woes of the rapidly failing radial lines, a new threat was developing in the United States. Gas companies, tire manufacturers, and car companies had been conspiring to buy up electric streetcar and railway lines just to close them down. Three such companies were convicted in the 1940s of anti trust violations. And while there is no positive proof that this happened here, the result was the same: cars, buses, and highways had replaced the radials.

Although most radial routes followed roads that have now been widened, you can still find many ghosts of the radial era today.

All Aboard

Despite its short duration, the Belt Line may be Toronto's best remembered ghost railway. Hundreds use it every day. Trains no longer run along it, but joggers do. Hikers walk it and cyclists cycle it.

Most of the eastern loop has become the Belt Line Trail, one of Toronto's most popular recreation trails. In two pieces, one segment lies south of Moore Avenue opposite the Mount Pleasant Cemetery. You enter the park at the site of the magnificent Moore Park Station, although no evidence of it remains. Following the demise of the Belt Line, the station survived as a house until 1945 when it burned down.

Jackson's Point station was a popular destination for York radial users. (MTL 976-21-B)

The trail follows the Belt Line roadbed south under the Heath Street bridge, the CPR bridge, and Governor's Road bridge. It emerges from the ravine, beside the Toronto Brick Works, now considered an historic site, and ends near the site of the former Rosedale station beside the Bayview Extension.

The other segment of the Belt Line Trail begins at Oriole Park near Avenue Road and follows the Belt Line northwesterly to Bathurst Street. As you pass beneath the bridge across Eglinton Avenue, you are passing the grounds of the former Eglinton Station. While the route south of Eglinton passes through shady woods, that north of Eglinton is pinched in a canyon of high-rise apartments.

There are other ghosts of the Belt Line. The railway bridge across Yonge Street south of Davisville was added by the CNR when it assumed ultimate ownership of the railway. On the east side of Yonge Street, near the corner of Merton, was the handsome storey-and-a-half Merton Street sta-

Toronto's "Belt Line" is more popular now than when it carried trains.

tion. The former Dominion Coal Company elevators still stand, preserved and re-painted, beside the Mount Pleasant bridge that once spanned the line. West of Bathurst Street, north of Eglinton Avenue, a short CNR siding still occupies the Belt Line right of way before linking onto the existing CNR line.

By contrast the western loop has been almost entirely obliterated by roads and houses. The only evidence of its existence lies in the orientation of the streets.

From the site of the former Davenport station south of St. Clair, the Belt Line followed what are now Terry Drive and Woolner Avenue to Jane Street and then influenced the curve on Florence Avenue (the Lambton station stood here) to St. Clair. It then paralleled Humbercrest to Old Mill Drive which follows the right of way itself. It then paralleled the South Kingsway south from Bloor Street to today's railway line near the Gardiner Expressway.

Of the Scarborough and Mimico radial lines, little remains. The Toronto Hunt Club remains a popular Kingston Road golf club, while Scarborough Heights survives only in the name of a residential street. The Halfway House, a pioneer hotel on Kingston Road which served as a station during radial days, was moved to Black Creek Pioneer Village. Radial stations survive in Port Credit, Port Stanley, Galt, and Paris.

The York and Guelph routes, however, have left much more for us to see.

Because urban sprawl has engulfed much of the route through Mississauga, the best place to start your exploration of the Guelph route is at Eldorado Park north of Steeles Avenue on Creditview Drive. Al-

though the roadbed is hard to find, the station yet survives as a pavilion. West of the park you can drive to Mississauga Road and follow it north to Huttonville. The roadbed lies beneath utility poles on the south wall of the Credit River.

The road bed continues along the valley and crosses Winston Churchill Blvd., again indicated by utility poles, south of Norval. The route once more has been obliterated by housing in the south end of Georgetown, although the large station survived for several decades as a bakery. It is now gone.

From a village with the evocative name of Limehouse to Guelph, the creators of the Guelph Radial Trail have convinced local

Much of the Guelph radial line is still traceable, in parts as a hiking trail, here as a residential lane.

landowners to allow hikers along about a third of the roadbed. In other sections the trail follows the bed closely. For the remaining third, landowners have refused hikers the permission necessary to hike the radial line.

West of Acton the abandoned right of way follows the shady banks of the Blue Springs Creek and the Eramosa River. Three kilometres south of Rockwood don't be surprised to hear the clanging of an interurban trolley and the clatter of steel wheels. In the Ontario Electric Railway Museum the old line comes to life as vintage trolleys follow the original roadbed for about a kilometre. You can board at the relocated Rockwood CNR station, and disembark at

a shelter that was once the radial flag station at Meadowvale.

In Eden Mills, a riverside community with houses and mill ruins built of local limestone, the right of way passes through a religious colony located on the south end of the village. The right of way, a path through the cedars, is not immediately clear. The station here was disassembled and moved to Main Street where it was reconstructed as a house. West of Eden Mills, a residential lane follows the right of way east from County Road 25 beneath a canopy of cedars. Hikers should follow the Guelph Radial Trail east from Watson Road in Guelph for one of the more natural treed portions of the route. At the end

John Moore designed an elaborate station he thought would be the focus of the suburb of Moore Park. (MTL T12185)

of the line you can still find a former radial power house. This two-storey structure, which also doubled as a station, is at the corner of James and Gordon Streets and is now an apartment building.

The other radial route worth following is the Toronto and York as it heads north from Newmarket to Sutton.

While the Newmarket station survived until 1988 as a pool room before being finally demolished, you may still find a couple of radial vestiges. In George Richardson Park, north of Davis Drive, you may discern the right of way as it skirts the east boundary of the park, before disappearing beneath new development. The most interesting relic, however, is the "rainbow bridge." Located on Queen Street between Main Street and Bayview Parkway, this arched culvert was once the bridge over which the radial trains crossed the Holland River. Although marked by an historic plaque and accessible from a parking lot, it is largely neglected and much decorated with graffiti.

The next visible vestige is at Queensville. Follow Queensville Road west of Leslie Street for one half kilometre to the Country Store: this is the location of the right of way. Utility poles that march across the field north of the road follow the roadbed. The station itself was moved to the

next lot east and converted to a house, whose bay window can be seen on the west side of the building.

You can return to the right of way at Roches Point on Lake Simcoe from where Metropolitan Road (Regional Road 78) follows the route for 15 kilometres east to Jackson's Point. Once a popular destination for Toronto beachgoers, there are a few structures here to tell the tale of the radial.

On the southeast corner of Kennedy Road at Willow Beach, a two-storey concrete house close to the road is the former Willow Beach power house and station. It is largely neglected, its history ignored. Drop in too on the Georgina Historic Museum, where two former flag stop shelters, with their red tile roofs, are now housed. And then in Sutton itself, marking the end of the line, is the station. Located at the corner of Dalton and High Streets, in its two storeys it now houses the Family Trust Real Estate offices.

Although the right of way that led from Oak Ridges to Schomberg is no longer visible, the Schomberg station still survives. If it closely resembles a house, the reason is that it originally was, before the railway purchased it to use as a station. Located on the north end of the main street and across from the feed mill, it has once more become a house.

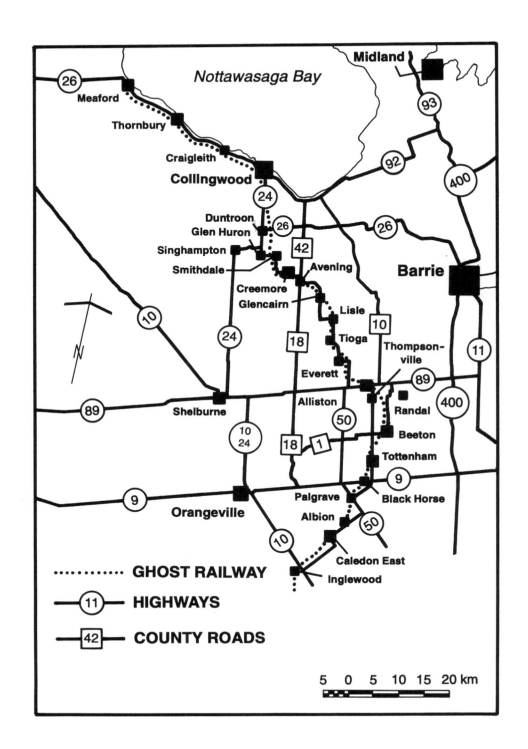

GHOST RAILWAY

HIGHWAYS

COUNTY ROADS

CHAPTER TWO

Something for Everyone: The Hamilton and Northwestern

Backgrounder

Of all Ontario's ghost railways, the abandoned roadbed of the Hamilton and Northwestern has the greatest variety of re-uses. From hiking trails along its southern portions to jogging routes further north, and even a genuine puffing heritage steam railway, the HNW has something for everyone.

Spurred by the arrival of the Great Western Railway in 1854, the promoters of what would become the HNW began with a more modest line that linked Hamilton with Port Dover on Lake Erie. Early railways were conveyors of people and products, mostly the latter, from Ontario's hinterlands to its ports. And the Hamilton and Port Dover was intended to be exactly that.

Its real potential, however, lay to the north. The Northern Railway, Ontario's first, realized that when it opened its line, the Ontario Simcoe and Huron, from Toronto to Aurora in 1853, and then to Allandale (now part of Barrie) and Collingwood. Eventually the HNW followed, snaking northward from Hamilton by crossing Hamilton Beach to Burlington, where it crossed the Great Western Railway, and to

Georgetown, where it crossed the Grand Trunk. From a point just north of Alliston it branched northwesterly to Collingwood, where it and the Northern Railway briefly operated rival stations.

One of the earliest portions to be abandoned was the line within Collingwood. When the Grand Trunk assumed control of the two lines in 1882, it saw no need for separate stations in the same place and retained the larger Northern station, removing the one built by the HNW. During the depression Port Dover declined as a port, and in 1935 the section between Jarvis and Port Dover was given up. It is somewhat surprising that it took until the 1950s for the railway to dispense with the section between Alliston and Collingwood (really a duplicate) except that some freight revenue still came from the villages along its route.

Beyond Collingwood the line to Meaford was built by the Northern Railway, not the HNW. This provides a continuous link for the backroad railway enthusiast to follow. While the records state that it was abandoned in 1985, it was actually given up on many years before that. The portion from Georgetown to Cheltenham was abandoned in 1975, and that from Cheltenham north to Beeton a decade later. The abandonment of the link between Beeton and Barrie in 1990, and between Jarvis and Hamilton, combined to complete the demise of the HNW.

All Aboard

Between Jarvis and Port Dover little remains of the right of way; much of it is now covered over with roads and other forms of development. Interestingly, the former Port Dover Union Station that served both this line and the Lake Erie and Northern branch from Simcoe, still stands. Relocated and truncated, it was nicely painted and much of its board and batten exterior left intact. Following an ignominious existence as a car wash, it became a craft shop, although its future remains by no means secure.

One of the most active sections of the HNW was that along Hamilton Beach. Inexpensive and close at hand, it was for many decades a popular summer retreat for Hamilton's steel workers and their families. Hotels and taverns like the Sportsman's Arms, the Dynes, and the Ocean House were household names to turn-of-the-century Hamiltonians. During the 1920s it became the preferred route of the CNR's fabled "silk trains" which rushed their heavily insured cargo virtually non-stop from the west coast to the fashion factories of the east coast.

The HNW comes back to life as the South Simcoe Heritage Railway in Tottenham.

Today Hamilton Beach is a residential suburb of Hamilton and Burlington. You can still see the former roadbed along the beach, and visit a relic of the area's heady summer resort days by dropping into the Dynes Tavern (which was so popular in its early days that the trains stopped at its back doors). Many drivers who are not too old still remember long and hot traffic jams in the days prior to the completion of the Skyway bridge when Hamilton Beach funneled the Queen Elizabeth Way traffic. The combined railway and automobile lift bridge, which seems at times — at least to fuming drivers — to remain suspended forever, replaced older swing and bascule bridges in 1958.

With the line still in use between Burlington and Georgetown, the continuous portion of this journey starts in Terra Cotta. Until the 1930s it was a busy brick manufacturing town that was originally known as Salmonville. Today Terra Cotta has become a popular destination for Sunday drivers to pause and enjoy a stroll by the Credit River, or (until recently) tea and scones at the widely known Terra Cotta Inn.

However, the rail fan will follow Isabella Street east from Winston Churchill Blvd. to the railway line, see above the trees the lonely chimney the last relic of the brick works, and hike along the Bruce Trail which follows the HNW easterly to Heritage Road, a distance of less than two kilometres. East of this point the regional government has decided that the privacy of prosperous property owners along the old rail line is of greater importance than the habits of hikers and has forced the Bruce Trail to follow busy roads.

However, by following Regional Road 9 east to Mississauga Road and driving north for two kilometres to the abandoned right of way at Mill Street, you come to one of the most impressive ruins anywhere in Ontario. The decrepit shells of the Interprovincial Brick Works lie on private lands behind a high chain-link fence. But by walking a few metres along the rail line you can look at them, photograph them, and imagine the times when a small company town and station stop were located here as well.

The brick works were acquired by Dofasco in 1958 and closed. Now owned by Brampton Brick, the ruins are preserved under a development agreement while the company extracts the red clay to make into bricks elsewhere. As a point of interest the 1914 battle scenes for the movie "The Wars" were filmed here.

Take Mill Street east to Cheltenham, with its old stone country store, and then drive north to Base Line Road which you follow east to Inglewood (stopping part way to gape in amazement at Ontario's "painted desert"). By foot or by car you can still see in the centre of Inglewood the overgrown railway station platform, the diamond that the HNW used to cross the CPR (then known as the Credit Valley Railway) and, nearby, the old brick railway hotel.

Just east of the 3rd Line West, south of Base Line Road, the Bruce Trail regains the rail line and follows it for nine kilometres through the surprisingly steep Caledon Hills. East of Highway 10 the trail crosses the long abandoned roadbed of the Toronto Grey and Bruce at a site known as Cardwell Junction. Early timetables indicate that a station with a restaurant stood here; later timetables, however, make no mention of it.

A short distance away and out of view on private property, lies the vague definition of the infamous horseshoe curve, a sharp bend on the Toronto Grey and Bruce (TGB) which claimed the lives of seven and injured 114 others, all Canadian National Exhibition bound excursionists. (This disaster is covered more fully in Chapter 8 on the TGB.)

Except for the presence of a church and scattered houses, no-one hiking the Bruce Trail along the right of way through Centreville would realize that it had once been the site of a station, woollen mill, hotel, and wagon factory.

While the railbed criss-crosses the various back roads between Centreville and Palgrave, perhaps the best way to enjoy it is to park in the hilly Albion Hills Conservation Area (entrance off Highway 50 south of Palgrave) and hike it. The line crosses the back portion of the area.

Although the Bruce Trail leaves the HNW here, the line remains very much in evidence in the middle of Palgrave, a town which retains a collection of historic structures. North of Palgrave, and especially noticeably as it passes under the Highway 9 bridge, the line parallels the CPR's still very active Sudbury branch. But it is at Tot-

tenham that this ghost railway comes back to life.

After seven years of legal wrangling and environmental hearings, the South Simcoe Heritage Railway puffed into existence in 1992. With its remarkable collection of steam engines and Credit Valley Railway coaches, it carries passengers along a short stretch of HNW line northward to Beeton, the elderly reliving memories of days of steam, the young experiencing it for the first time. Beeton was once an important railway town, although you'd never know it today. Tracks, a tower, a coal dock, and a large two-storey station, which was designed by the Northern and Pacific Railway

The abandoned line west of Collingwood allows trail users to pass by Craigleith,
one of Ontario's most attractive little stattions

and which stood until the 1960s all these have vanished.

Drive north of Beeton almost to the intersection of the 11th line and the 10th sideroad (which you are on). The hidden fork of the line known as "Alimill" or "Beeton Junction" (a name that has survived on a local school) marks the branching of the line northeast to Barrie and northwest to Collingwood. Only recently abandoned, the Barrie branch is still very evident, while the Collingwood branch is less noticeable.

Five kilometres to the northeast, on the Barrie branch, Randall "Station" consisted of a platform and a mail hook. The ticket agent lived in the house that still stands today sporting the name "Randall Station."

Then the fresh cinders of the Barrie branch pass through prosperous farm lands, through historic Cookstown, where the station survives as a remodelled house east of the roadbed, to Thornton, and then Vine, where the station also survives as a house, before joining the CNR's main line in Barrie.

Before it attained its junction with the Northern railway at Allandale, the HNW had its own stations both in Allandale, near the corner of Essa Road and Baldwin, and in downtown Barrie near Sofia and Bayfield Streets. This may come as somewhat of a surprise to Barrie residents today, for subsequent development has covered over all evidence that a railway line was ever there.

While the bed of the Barrie branch into Allandale is clearly evident, the main line to Collingwood has all but vanished. It lies uncelebrated, forgotten, and now hard to find. It does nonetheless lead you through a string of historic rural towns and some of the hilliest countryside in central Ontario.

Crossing the south end of Alliston the HNW roadbed passes one of the town's most interesting heritage structures, the "Co-op" feed mill. Located at Tupper and Paris Streets south of the main street, this four-storey brick building sports three large towers. However, further west at Tupper and Albert Streets the station grounds have long been vacant, although the ticket wicket is preserved in the Simcoe County Museum.

To reach Everett, the first station stop west of Alliston, follow Highway 89 west to County Road 13 and turn north. Once a busy shipper of grain and potatoes, Everett is now an attractive residential community. Originally located some distance away, Everett's businesses moved to trackside when the rails arrived. Today you cannot find even the right of way, much less the tracks. Wales Avenue, which leads to a new subdivision, marks the former location of both.

Eight kilometres further north the county road ends at Lisle, another town that boomed with the coming of the railway. Although it had a station (which outlasted the demise of the line as a Legion Hall, only to burn down later) and a water tank, all evidence of its railway heritage has vanished.

To reach Glencairn, the next station stop on the HNW, follow County Road 12 west to Airlie and turn north. Here you will find the only effort to preserve anything of the HNW's history on the entire section, and it's not much. Just before you reach the stop sign, look on the west side of the road. The garage bearing the old station name board is the freight shed portion of that station.

From Glencairn drive west to County Road 42 and then north to Avening. "Station Road" leads down a private land and ends short of where once stood the station, a grain elevator, and stock yards. Other than the name of the street, and a one-time railway hotel at the corner, Avening's railway heritage too has vanished.

Creemore is the largest village on the route between Alliston and Collingwood. With its "smallest" jail (one block east of the main street), and its preserved downtown core, Creemore has demonstrated concern for its heritage. Had its attractive station not burned in 1955 that too might have become part of the heritage preservation efforts. So now, there is no sign that there was even a railway here. The IGA store sits squarely on the former right of way.

While the railway heritage between Creemore and Collingwood may be lacking, the scenery is not. And by following the old railway roadbed, you will share the beauty that the HNW passengers enjoyed from the windows of their passenger coaches.

Follow County Road 9 west from Creemore for about four kilometres to Nottawasaga Concession Road 6 and turn north. The route follows the treed banks of the Mad River, part of the route on the roadbed itself. It leads you to Smithdale, at the first crossroads, the site of the Glen Huron station. However, all evidence of the the Old HNW has been ploughed under the farm fields.

Less than three kilometres further west loom the cliffs of the Niagara Escarpment and the scenic village of Glen Huron itself. Tucked into the steep walls of the Mad River valley it is home to the Hamilton feed mill, as it has been for nearly a century.

Duntroon lies about six kilometres further north. About one kilometre east of the village core on Highway 91, you can see the

right of way carved from the hillside on the south side of the highway. The grounds of the long vanished station and grain elevator lie along a "no exit" road on the north side. A private home there dates from steam days and may have housed the station agent. The station itself was a large board and batten structure with a gable over the bay window.

From here, north into Collingwood, the vestiges of the HNW are scant. The views over Georgian Bay from Highway 24, however, more than compensate, taking in fields, forests, and blue waters, and make for some of this area's more scenic driving.

The HNW entered Collingwood on Walnut Street, seven blocks west of the main street(Hurontario Street). At the corner of Second Street the line briefly had its own station and engine house, until it moved into the facilities of the Grand Trunk (formerly the Northern) Railway. Of the factories and mills that once lined the HNW route, only the building that housed the Cameron and Shipley flour mill on the north side of Highway 26 survives.

East of Hurontario Street, the main drag, at the corner of St. Paul, the old Grand Trunk station stood until 1997 when it was dismantled. Having served several years as a museum, the aging structure proved too costly to upgrade.

The North Grey line carried both the Grand Trunk and the HNW westward along First Street (Highway 26) to Thornbury and Meaford. Today it has become the popular 32-kilometre-long Georgian Trail. It could have been the dream route for what is now the South Simcoe Railway society. Had they succeeded in placing their steam excursions along this route they would have provided North America with its most scenic heritage railway. The objections of the local landowners prevailed, however, and the project was shelved.

But the roadbed is still there. You can hike it, you can bike it, you can jog it, or you can cross country ski it. You can even drive beside it. Whatever method you choose, you will find the blue waters of Georgian Bay tossing to the north, and the forested summits of the Blue Mountains looming above you to the south.

Further on, the delightful little red station at Craigleith with its tower and its detailed woodwork still stills on site, having served for many years as a popular local restaurant. It was one of the first stations in Ontario to be preserved and re-used. The trail then crosses the highway and follows the shoreline into Thornbury, the former station there now standing as a house at the corner of King and Alma Streets. A cooling lakeside park and marina mark the end of "rail" in Meaford. Although the station has long been removed, a freight shed has managed to survive.

In the heyday of rail travel, families reunited at the station. (CN)

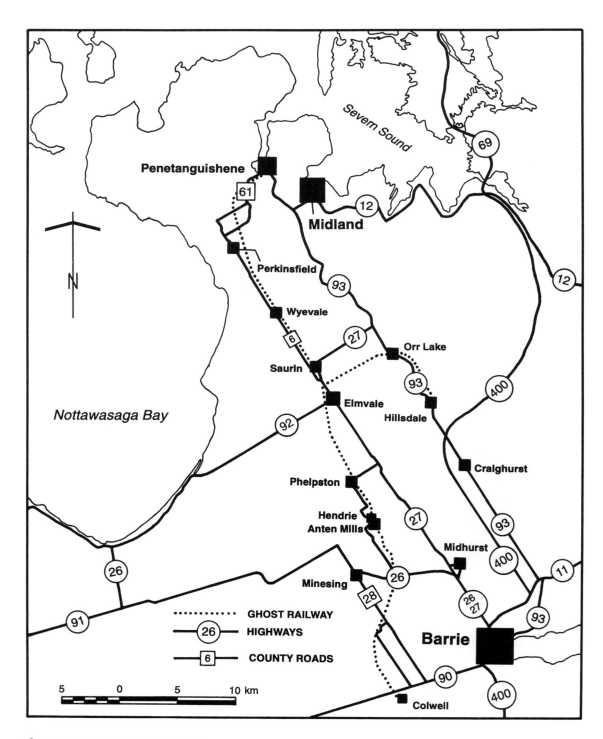

Severn Sound

Penetanguishene

Perkinsfield

Wyevale

Saurin

Midland

Orr Lake

Nottawasaga Bay

Elmvale

Hillsdale

Craighurst

Phelpston

Hendrie
Anten Mills

Midhurst

Minesing

Barrie

Colwell

.... GHOST RAILWAY

(26) HIGHWAYS

[6] COUNTY ROADS

5   0   5   10 km

N

CHAPTER THREE

The North Simcoe: A Little Line

Backgrounder

During the 1870s, Ontario's railway builders began to pay more attention to the busy little ports on Georgian Bay. As Ontario's southern forests became depleted, the loggers made their way into the lush pine stands that ringed Georgian Bay. But to bring that lumber to Ontario's urban markets and those in the northern United States required railways.

Among the first were the Hamilton and Northwestern and the Northern. But both of these went to the same place: Collingwood. In fact the two merged in 1882. However, two ports further east provided better shelter and therefore better potential for sawmills; these were Penetanguishene and Midland. While the Midland Railway came from the east, the Northern with its line through Barrie was already close and needed only a short branch line to reach Penetanguishene.

Although the North Simcoe was born under a seemingly independent name, the Northern took it over almost immediately. In 1879 it opened from Colwell Junction on the Northern Railway west of Barrie to Penetang and Midland. Six years later the Grand Trunk, extending its steel empire gobbled up both the Northern and the North Simcoe.

For 95 years the line fed the needs of the Grand Trunk and later the CNR. After the CNR pulled its last passenger coach from the route in the 1950s, it continued to haul lumber and some manufactured products. In 1975 the CNR abandoned it entirely. A short stub penetrated as far as Hendrie for another eleven years, then it too was lifted, and the line fell silent. Today most of the line is maintained as a snowmobile trail, alive with the roar of snow machines in the winter, or the more silent footfalls of hikers and equestrians in the summer. The route leads you to the small villages, ports, and hills of a little appreciated part of Ontario, the territory of the North Simcoe.

All Aboard

Colwell Junction, ten kilometres west of Barrie, is the start of your expedition. Now overwhelmed by Barrie's urban sprawl, the little railway village harbours a few vestiges of its railway junction days. Although the station and other buildings have vanished, a walk west down the overgrown right of way of the Northern (where rail was still in place at the time of writing) will bring you to the name board and the location of the branch. Only a small railway residence survives amid the trees on the north side of the track.

The line straight ahead is the old main line to Collingwood, that of the Northern, and the branch to the north is the start of the North Simcoe. Colwell Junction is on Essa Concession 9, south of Highway 90.

From Colwell Junction the line heads north to the foreboding Minesing Swamp. Here it skirts the hills that overlook the swamp and passes the rebuilt remains of the Willow Creek Depot. Built during the war of 1812 as a supply depot for troops and guns en route to the Georgian Bay, the small log fort was in ruins by 1830, and soon vanished altogether. During the 1970s the Nottawasaga Valley Conservation Authority began to reconstruct the depot as a tourist attraction. But local vandals remained one step ahead of them, defacing the buildings and littering the site with garbage. Even the historic plaque has been stolen.

To follow the line and visit the site of Willow Creek, turn north from Highway 90 onto Vespra Concession 10, or drive north on County Road 28 and follow the orange and blue directional markers. From

Although the station is long gone, the Wyevale name board has been rescued and marks the spot where the station once stood.

Willow Creek Depot drive east to County Road 28 and north to Minesing. While a few old buildings remain in the village of Minesing, all signs of the station, three kilometres to the east, have long vanished. You may still see the ruins of a freight ramp, however, now overgrown rubble. The line emerges from the swamp here to become a public trail. The line then continues past farm land for six kilometres to Anten Mills and the site of the tiny Hendrie Station. This bungalow-sized depot managed to last until the late 1970s and was the last station on the line to survive.

Drive east from Minesing Station to Vespra Concession 7/8 and follow it north to a T intersection at Highway 27 and turn east. Another kilometre brings you to the site of Hendrie station. Turn north here and drive to another T intersection with Flos Concession 1/2. Drive east to the first sideroad north. Here the road and right of way parallel each other into the old Irish village of Phelpston three kilometres to the north.

From here the old railway line crosses flat farmlands for eight kilometres to Elmvale. Until the railway arrived, Elmvale was little more than a farm post office. The station, however, made the place the centre for the region, and Elmvale boomed. The station, although simple in style, was one of the largest on the line. Board and batten in construction, it had a simple roof line and

It's difficult to conceive why railway companies would demolish its attractive stations, like this former Grand Trunk station on the NS line in Penetanguishene.

no architectural embellishments. Nevertheless, it attracted feed mills and warehouses, one of which still survives and can be seen on the north side of Highway 92 west of the present village.

From Elmvale a branch line, known as the Flos Tramway, swung easterly bending around the north side of Orr lake and down into the mill village of Hillsdale on Highway 93. No trace remains of this local curiosity, although a picturesque old mill and hotel still cling to existence in Hillsdale. Drive north from Elmvale on Highway 27 for a little over two kilometres and turn onto County Road 6. Here the old line ventures beside the road to Saurin, a hamlet of modern homes that owes its name to James Saurin, one of the early railway builders. Two kilometres from Saurin, a sideroad to the east passes beneath an old railway overpass and marks the location of the Tay Tramway that led to Midland. Long abandoned, all vestiges of the branch have vanished save for bridge abutments south of Wyebridge on Highway 93.

But it is at the similarly named Wyevale (both are named from the Wye River on which they lie), that you will find a local effort to celebrate the heritage of the railway that gave life to the village. Prior to the railway the place didn't even appear in the business directories, but when rail reached town, Wyevale flourished. Look in the roadside park on the east for the station name board and a plaque commemorating the construction of the line. A small railway cabin also survives on the east side of the park.

The line hugs the road for another four kilometres before angling away into the forests and fields. You will encounter the route again at the site of the Leclerc Memorial Park one kilometre east of Perkinsfield on County Road 25. The village is the heart of a small but vibrant francophone community and contains an attractive catholic church that dominates the intersection.

Continue north from Perkinsfield to Lefaivre Corners and drive east to Penetanguishene. As you enter the village from the west on Robert Street, you will cross the right of way which then descends to follow the water to the foot of the main street, Penetanguishene Road. All vestiges of the line, the station, and other buildings have been swept away to create an open park. The station which survived into the early 1970s was a typical Grand Trunk style with gables over the bay and porte-cochere.

The parks and a marina give you a chance to scan the cliff-lined harbour and sniff the breeze from the cool waters of Georgian Bay. North of Penetang, the 1812 naval establishment is one of Ontario's most prized historic treasures.

The NS depot at Elmvale was typical of most
built along the line. (SCA)

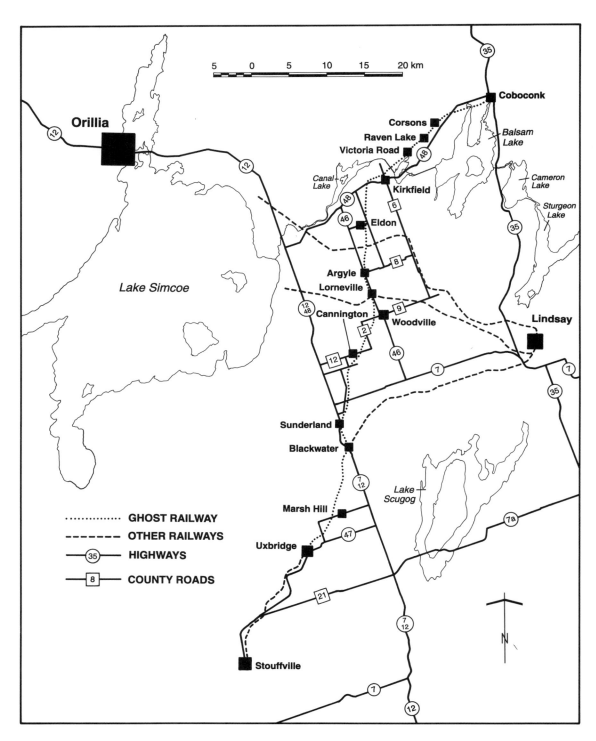

Scale: 5 0 5 10 15 20 km

Orillia

Lake Simcoe

Coboconk

Corsons

Raven Lake

Balsam Lake

Victoria Road

Canal Lake

Cameron Lake

Kirkfield

Eldon

Sturgeon Lake

Argyle

Lorneville

Cannington

Woodville

Lindsay

Sunderland

Blackwater

Lake Scugog

Marsh Hill

Uxbridge

.... GHOST RAILWAY

- - - - - - OTHER RAILWAYS

—(35)— HIGHWAYS

—[8]— COUNTY ROADS

N

Stouffville

CHAPTER FOUR

The Toronto and Nipissing: The Kawartha Connection

Backgrounder

The Toronto and Nipissing Railway, the creation in part of George Laidlaw and William Gooderham (one of the founders of the magnificent Gooderham and Worts industrial complex in east-end Toronto), was a relatively short line that stretched northeast of Toronto, through the towns of Stouffville and Uxbridge to Coboconk, and then stopped. That portion of the line between Uxbridge and Toronto remains in place, although is little used, while the northeastern end lies abandoned. Along it lie portions of traceable roadbed, a few stations, and ghostly ruins.

Originally a narrow gauge railway, i.e. the rails were 3 1/2' apart rather than the now universal 4' 8 1/2", the line opened to traffic as far as Uxbridge in 1871. The following year it reached Coboconk, a distant mill town that would remain its terminus. With the evolution of a spider's web of rail lines across central Ontario, two points on the T&N became important junctions: Blackwater Junction and Lorneville Junction. At Blackwater the line split, one section going to Lindsay, the other to Coboconk. Lorneville was an important crossing with

the Midland Railway, a line that ran from Port Hope to Midland.

Because passenger traffic remained light, the line depended for most of its revenue upon the sawmills and the Kirkfield quarry. Following the closing of the quarry in 1965, the section between Cannington and Coboconk was abandoned. That between Blackwater and Woodville, however, would remain in place for another twenty years.

All Aboard

A good place to start your exploration is Uxbridge. It was here that the grand opening ceremonies took place in 1871 and where you will still find an interesting station with a conical roof atop the waiting room, a feature that earned the style the nickname the "witch's hat" style. Now a museum, until 1992 it was a residence. From Uxbridge to Blackwater the route follows the shallow swampy valley of the Blackwater River, past a vanished pioneer community with the somewhat contradictory name of Marsh Hill, to Blackwater Junction. The road to follow, however, is Highway 47 easterly to Highways 7/12 and then north.

Blackwater Junction's industries grew to include grain elevators, a sawmill, and a busy stockyard from which farmers could ship their livestock to Toronto. The station itself was an interesting structure with bay windows and platforms on each side. Inside were waiting rooms, a ticket office, baggage rooms, and a restaurant.

The station stood east of the highway in the swamp below the village. Shortly after passenger service stopped in 1962 the station came down. Although there remains little to see of the station grounds or of the right of way, you can still visit the village.

The highway itself bypasses the village completely, but a sideroad to the east which was formerly the village's main street has a few railway-age homes. However, the site is attracting country dwellers, and newer housing has nearly obliterated Blackwater's railway aura.

A short distance north of Blackwater is Sunderland. With the arrival of the railway in 1874 it grew from a sleepy crossroads hamlet to a bustling industrial and commercial centre with over thirty businesses, a sawmill, and a co-op. While the railway line lies at the bottom of a short hill just east of where the highway turns north, the town's main point of interest for the rail fan lies in the attractive brick structures on

The Lorneville station once stood at the junction of the T&N and the Midland Railways. (CIHB)

the main street. Most owe their existence to a railway that is gone and almost entirely forgotten.

Cannington is east of Highway 12 on County Road 12. The site of sawmills as early as 1833, Cannington was already prospering, but when the railway came to town the place boomed and several more streets were laid out. Cameron, Shedden, McCrae, and Elliot Streets were all named after prominent railway officials. To find the overgrown station grounds follow Shedden Street south from the commercial core to St. John. While the yards, the grounds, and the industries have all vanished, you may yet see one of the former railway hotels on the corner of these two streets. As you re-

turn to the main street via Peace Street, you will see, behind the Community Centre, the "Cannington" station. In front is a former caboose.

Despite the name board this is the station that stood not in Cannington, but in Mount Albert well to the west. The actual Cannington station, a simpler structure, burned down in the 1960s. In fact, most of the stations along this section of the line were simple in design, single storey with a plain roof line. Some even lacked the bay window where the station operators would sit.

At Cannington the roadbed leaves the swampy banks of the Blackwater River and ventures northeasterly across fields as a dry

The Kirkfield station has survived unchanged since the last train called.

weather local "road." Through Woodville, on County Road 46, the right of way is nearly invisible as it passes along the west end of the village. Originally the centre for a Scottish farm colony, and almost called Otaga, it boomed with the coming of the railway. It has reverted to being the centre for the surrounding community and most vestiges of its railway heritage have vanished.

Lorneville, on the other hand, three kilometres north of Woodville on County Road 46, was the junction between Toronto and Nipissing and the Midland Railways and was all railway. As the historical atlas for Ontario County noted at the time, "Lorneville has grown up around the junction of the railways where a good deal of grain is bought. The population is mostly composed of railway men and their families. Near the station and other station buildings are two hotels, shops and the post office." At the crossing of the two tracks, know in railway terminology as a "diamond," stood the station with its small tower atop the corner bay window.

While many newer houses have been built in the community, you can still discern some of the vanishing railway heritage. Just north of the abandoned store and gas station, the Midland right of way remains visible as a slight depression to the east of County Road 46. While the right of way is indiscernible to the west of the road, a couple of streets lead to what were the former station grounds and hotel sites. The location now lies on private property and is so overgrown as to be no longer visible. The station itself, however, survives. Rescued by a local resident, it now sits behind a farmhouse about 100 metres to the north.

From Lorneville the roadbed is scarcely traceable as it follows the farm fields on the west side of County Road 46. Argyle, three

kilometres north of Lorneville, was the next station stop, the grounds located a short distance west of the intersection. Although the station has been gone for several decades, the roadbed is still visible as private lane. Argyle retains a few railway-age structures and some that are older. These include a former hotel near the right of way, and at the intersection, an early general store and one-time blacksmith shop.

As you continue north on County Road 46 you will pass the CPR's former Eldon station, now a house, which nevertheless retains it distinctive station features. It sits on the long abandoned Georgian Bay and Seaboard route, included in Chapter Six with the Midland Railway. The right of way then crosses the highway and continues north to Eldon, now a small collection of houses along the second farm road north of Argyle and about three kilometres east of the highway. Drive north from Eldon to Highway 48 and continue east towards Kirkfield. The right of way crosses the highway again about two kilometres east and marks the site of a now vanished community called Portage Road.

Perhaps the most interesting community on the old line is Kirkfield. Predating the advent of the railway by about forty years, the place boomed when the rails reached town. The village's economic mainstay today is the retail trade along the highway. Its most historic building is the summer residence of the railroading MacKenzie family, William MacKenzie being a co-founder of the Canadian Northern Railway network. The railway itself passed through town about 1.5 kilometres north of the highway. While the right of way is merely an overgrown mound, the original station still survives, its name board in place, at the site of Cross Construction.

From this location a branch line swung north to serve the famous Kirkfield quarry. One of Ontario's busiest, the limestone quarry contained its own village, with thirty company houses, and a narrow gauge railway. Its production often exceeded thirty carloads a day and became the largest revenue generator of the railway. The closing of the quarry in the early 1960s spelled the end of the railway.

Near the station a small freight shed marks the alignment of the quarry branch. Otherwise the quarry, about five kilometres north, is fenced off and the traces of the quarry village and railway have been removed. One of the old saddle-back locomotives, however, was rescued and is on display at the Simcoe County museum near Barrie. Near the site of the quarry you will find one of Ontario's most intriguing transportation structures, the Kirkfield lift lock. One of only a few in the world, and along with the Peterborough lift lock, unique in North America, it was built in 1904 and lifts boats travelling the Trent Canal some twenty metres into the air. The site now contains a popular picnic and viewing area.

You can reach Victoria Road, the next station stop, by driving east from the lock for five kilometres, or by returning to Kirkfield and following Highway 48 east to County Road 35 and driving north. While Kirkfield was born before and lived after the railway,

The main street of Victoria Road shows that it has seen better times.

Victoria Road lived and died with it. The site of sawmills and sidings, the place now resembles a ghost town. The shops, churches, and homes date from the days of rail and have changed little since. Most of the old businesses are shuttered. An enterprise calling itself the "Museum of Temporary Art" occupies the rambling old general store, while the station still stands, altered somewhat to become a dwelling, the grounds embellished with railway memorabilia.

Another of the ghosts of the Toronto and Nipissing lies a short distance east of Victoria Road. It is the shell of the short-lived Raven Lake cement plant. Deep deposits of marl on the bottom of Raven Lake and access via the T&N attracted the company to the site where in 1904 it built a large stone plant. But after just ten years of production peaking at 700 barrels of cement a day with a labour force of 200, the company was the victim of an early form of free trade in the guise of cheaper American cement, and it closed.

Its ghosts lurk in the woods on Raven Road about one kilometre north of Highway 48. Although it sits behind two sturdy chain-link fences on private property, you can easily view the extensive roofless stone ruins from the railway right of way a few yards east of the road. You can then put yourself in the train engineer's seat and continue for 1.3 kilometres along the old railroadbed, now an unmaintained dry weather lane, to a point where it becomes no longer passable.

The next location on the line was Corson's. Named after John Corson, manger of the nearby Gooderham and Worts timber limits, it contained no more than a siding. Amid a few homes, old and new, the site of the roadbed and siding are scarcely discernible.

At the end of the line, and of Highway 48, stands Coboconk. With the arrival of the Toronto and Nipissing, Coboconk until then a landing on Balsam Lake, bloomed into a busy steamer stop, popular with tourists and the site of a large steam sawmill. The building of the roads to cottage country during the 1950s assured its viability as a recreational town, and the closing of the railway in the 1960s had little impact.

While the sawmill and the timber have vanished, the station was moved in 1997 to nearby Legion Park and preserved as a museum. The two-storey portion of the structure represents the original station, while the single-storey section was a later addition.

Although it was one of the shorter lines in Ontario, the Toronto and Nipissing has more than its share of railway relics.

The T&N's Coboconk station for years was part of a building supply office.

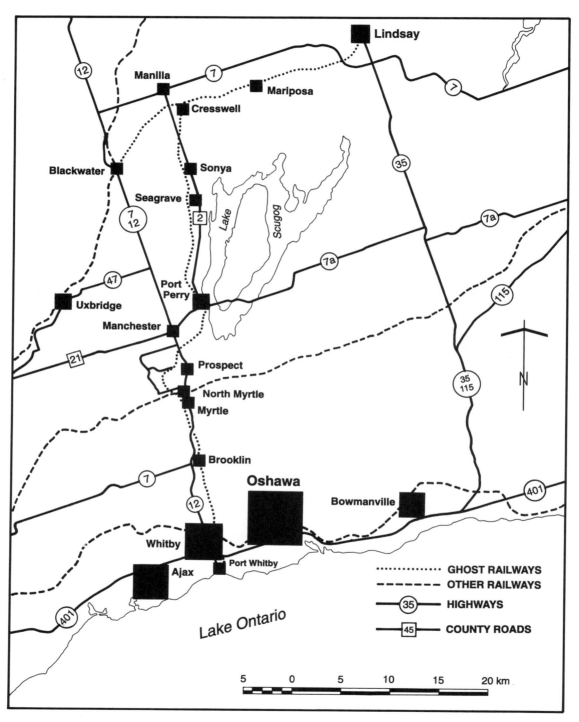

Lindsay

Manilla

Mariposa

Cresswell

Blackwater

Sonya

Seagrave

Lake Scugog

Uxbridge

Port Perry

Manchester

Prospect

North Myrtle

Myrtle

Brooklin

Oshawa

Bowmanville

Whitby

Ajax

Port Whitby

Lake Ontario

N

.... GHOST RAILWAYS
- - - - - - OTHER RAILWAYS
—(35)— HIGHWAYS
—[45]— COUNTY ROADS

5   0   5   10   15   20 km

CHAPTER FIVE

The Whitby Port Perry and Lindsay:
Gone and Forgotten

Backgrounder

During the early years of railway mania, rivalry was rampant among Lake Ontario's port communities. Every port wanted rail access to the hinterland and most got it; Whitby was one such port.

Although the town is not on the lake, it was only a short distance inland from Port Whitby. From the lake the railway line drove toward Whitby and its junction with the Grand Trunk. By 1871 it would reach Port Perry and six years later, Lindsay. In later years it crossed the Canadian Northern six kilometres north of Whitby, before passing through Brooklin, and Myrtle (the junction with the Ontario and Quebec), and entering Port Perry. From Port Perry the line continued north through Seagrave to its junction with the Midland Railway at Cresswell or Manilla Junction.

Although the right of way is all but invisible along most of its route, it passes through some pastoral countryside, country towns, and even offers up a couple of stations.

All Aboard

What better place to start your route along the Whitby Port Perry and Lindsay (WPPL)than at the former Whitby Junction station. Built by the Grand Trunk Railway around 1903, it stood at the corner of Brock Road and Highway 401 until 1973. Then with the closing of the station, and the arrival of GO Transit, the local arts community bought the building and moved it one half kilometre south to the corner of Victoria and Henry. Restored to its Grand Trunk colours of green and grey and with its twin turrets and ornate woodwork, it is one of Ontario's most photogenic stations.

If you drive south from the station on Brock Road until you come to Water Street, you can still see where the railway began. Here, in what is today a park, the WPPL trains began puffing northward. Although no longer used, there is still some rail in the park. Throughout Whitby itself, the tracks have been removed and replaced with new stores, houses, and parking lots.

The simpler downtown Whitby station lasted until 1971, and the engine house was re-used for car repairs until the 90s. Today, all is vacant land, with no evidence or celebration of the old railway.

Highway 12 is your road to follow from Whitby to Port Perry. North of Whitby, country homes and strip development have sprawled along the roads, obliterating most evidence of the railway. In the community of Brooklin about twelve kilometres north, drive east on Regional Road 3 to Anderson Street. The trees lining this road are set back several metres from the roadside, a widening that reflects the railway right of way.

Six and one half kilometres further along Highway 12 brings you to the first of two Myrtles. In the pre-railway days the dreadful road conditions meant that farmers had to have all their services close at hand in one of the thousands of tiny crossroads hamlets that dotted early Ontario. Myrtle began life as one such hamlet. But the arrival of the railways changed all that as stores and factories gravitated to trackside, leaving the crossroads settlements to wither and often become ghost towns.

The first Myrtle did get its railway line, the WPPL in 1871. The station was simple, a single-storey wooden structure that lacked even a bay window for the operator. But it vanished years ago and there is little to see.

The Whitby Junction Grand Trunk station was saved and restored by a local art gallery.

The right of way lies 400 metres west of the highway on Myrtle Road. The second of the two Myrtles, known as Myrtle Station, outgrew the parent with the arrival of the Ontario and Quebec Railway. While the station and the grain elevators are now gone, the community remains the larger of the two.

The next "station" was a mere siding and flag stop known as High Point Station. To reach the site watch for Scugog Road 2, about three kilometres north of Myrtle and follow it to the Smith Sideroad. Take the side road north 800 metres to High Point Road and turn west. The station sat in the vicinity of the High Point farm. While the track behind has been ploughed under, a gap visible in a ridge at the back of the farm marks the cut through which the tracks were laid.

Return to Highway 12 and continue north, passing Scugog Line 3, and drive to a pair of houses on the east side of the highway. The large white house at the end of the treed lane marks the site of the Manchester station, and was a railway-related building itself, likely a hotel. From Manchester (the village is three kilometres north of the "station" at Highway 7A) drive into Port Perry. Don't bother looking for the right of way until you reach Port Perry: it has been buried beneath fields and houses.

In Port Perry turn north from Highway 7A onto Water Street. Drive beside the

By contrast, Whitby's downtown station was much simpler. (DS)

lakeside park until you come to a flower shop. You are looking at what once was the Port Perry railway station. Moved from its original site just across the street in the park (you can still make out the foundations), it has been substantially renovated. However, from the parking lot behind the store you can see the operator's bay window and the overall shape of the station itself. The feed mill north of the park, dates from the railway and is a landmark. Behind the mill a short street leads to a path through the Port Perry Wildlife Park and marks the former railway causeway. While the line south of Port Perry was abandoned in 1941, that north of town was lifted in 1937 and is slightly harder to trace.

From Port Perry follow the Regional Road 2 north for about twelve kilometres to Seagrave and enter town. Seagrave has retained much of its rural character, and its most interesting structures are the Seagrave Country Store and the Ocean House Hotel. The long abandoned right of way is now maintained as a recreational trail.

The railway and the road continue north through the hamlet of Sonya, with its historic church and century-old houses, to Cresswell. Cresswell is all railway and marks the once busy junction of the WPPL with the Midland Railway. In 1883, the latter — a burgeoning company — took over both the WPPL and the Toronto and Nipissing just to the west,

and built a short link between the two. It called its junction at Cresswell "Manilla Junction" and that with the Nipissing "Blackwell Junction." While the linking trackage between the WPPL and the Nipissing was built westward from Manilla Junction by the Midland, the trackage eastward into Lindsay was built originally by the WPPL.

In Cresswell look on the south side of the road for an old red brick building. Here stands the former railway hotel, now a private home, but once the site of rowdy parties involving railway gangs. Cresswell Road was built on the right of way and follows it north a short distance to the site of the railway junction. The foundations of the station lie to the east. The rails were lifted from the road bed of the "Midland" in 1992 and the right of way is now maintained as a recreational trail.

Continue east from Cresswell to Victoria Road 6 where you can find the site of the Mariposa station. Once a busy cattle and grain shipping spot in the midst of prosperous farm country, it still retains the freight building. The large wooden station, however, was torn down in 1967.

The fresh right of way continues east into Lindsay, crossing under the Highway 7 bridge to join the original main line of Midland at Durham and Victoria Streets. (The railway vestiges of Lindsay are described in more detail in Chapter 22 on the Victoria Railway.)

Port Perry's station was moved across the street to become a flower shop.

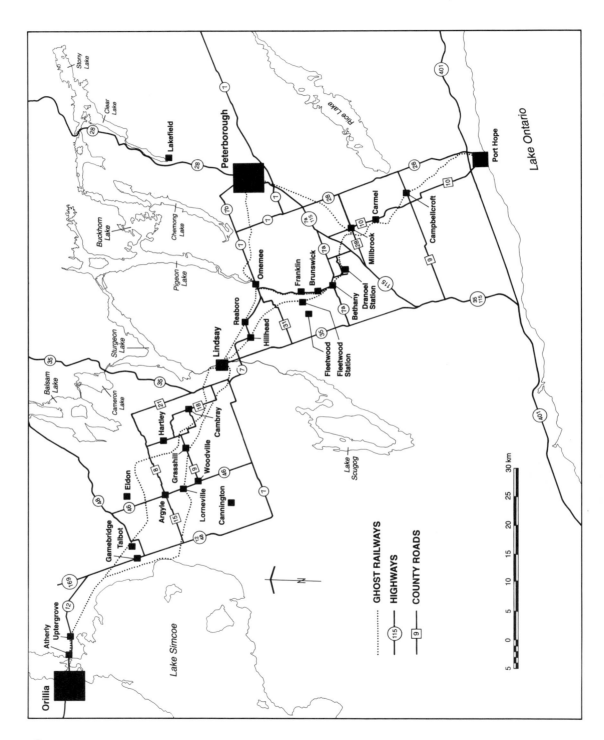

CHAPTER SIX

Between the Lakes: The Midland Railway

Backgrounder

Of all the railway rivalries that developed between the ports on Lake Ontario, that between Port Hope and Cobourg was the fiercest. In the early 1850s both wanted to be the first to build a railway to a then booming mill town on the Otonabee River known as Ashburnham, later to be called Peterborough. Although Port Hope had a charter as early as 1854 to construct a line called the Port Hope and Peterborough, Cobourg began building first, a move that doomed Port Hope's chances.

Conceding Peterborough to their rivals, the Port Hope interests decided to build instead to Midland on Georgian Bay and called their venture the Midland Railway of Canada. They did not forget Peterborough entirely, however, and eventually built a branch line from Millbrook to that destination. By 1879 the "Midland" could claim a main line from Port Hope to Lindsay, Orillia, and Midland, with a branch line through Peterborough to Lakefield.

Throughout the 1880s, in order to counter CPR expansion in southern Ontario, the Grand Trunk urged the Midland to gobble up lines like the Toronto and Nipissing, the Whitby Port Perry and Lindsay, and the Grand Junction. In a few years the Midland had expanded its network from 145 miles to more than 450. But the sudden expansion was too much for the little line and soon after, the Grand Trunk swooped down and added the Midland to its own empire.

All Aboard

This route covers the old Midland main line from Port Hope to Orillia, as well as the branch line to Peterborough.

You will not be in a hurry to leave Port Hope. The preserved 19th century downtown invites a leisurely stroll, as does the park in front of the city hall beside the Ganaraska River. Now refurbished, the Grand Trunk station squats at the end of Hayward Street, west of John. One of the smaller versions of the Grand Trunk's early stone arch stations it has remained in continuous railway use since 1856, a record proud Port Hope residents claim is the longest in Canada.

While the early Midland Railway offices are gone (they were just south of the city hall), there is still a Midland Railway "station" in town. On Walton Street (the main street) look for Lent's Travel. Then look down the laneway beside it. Here were the railway station and platform, and the second opening for a door was for the waiting room. You can also see the indentation for the old name board, as well as a still extant mile board sign. (While following the abandoned Canadian Northern line in the next chapter you will encounter Port Hope's grand old Canadian Northern station.

Following one of the more elaborate patterns adopted by this line, it was occupied for several years by the Ontario Ministry of Transportation. You can find it at Ontario and Howard Streets.)

Your route out of Port Hope leads you north up Cavan Street. Near the foot of Bedford Street look for the remains of the old bridge that carried the railway across the river. The line then went beside the road to Molson Street. At about this point you can see the abutments that held the Canadian Northern bridge. While the railway right of way follows the banks of the Ganaraska, you must travel east on Molson to reach Ontario Street or Highway 28.

The offices of the Midland Railway stood in Port Hope.

With stretches abandoned between Port Hope and Millbrook in 1957 and to Peterborough seven years later, the Midland has left little trace along these southern reaches. However the route does lead you across old Ontario, through villages that predate the railway, villages with historic hotels and general stores. It leads you past family farms that carry on operations started in many cases by the pioneer ancestors of today's occupants.

Continue north on Highway 28 to the 4th Line and turn west. Three kilometres leads you to the right of way. At this point the Ganaraska Hiking Trail turns on to the abandoned right of way and traces it northward for 4.5 kilometres. The first road that

it crosses is the site of a small flag station named "Quay's." At the 6th Line the trail leaves the right of way to follow the farm roads. You can of course drive to the same location. Continue west for another two kilometres on the 4th Line and turn north. After three kilometres, at the first crossroads, you can find the site of the Perrytown "station" by turning right and driving a few metres.

Return to the intersection and continue north. Two kilometres takes you past Fudge's mill and on to Regional Road 9. One half kilometre east is the railway hamlet of Campbellcroft. The settlement grew when the Midland built a station and was originally known as Garden Hill Station.

Millbrook was the junction of the Midland main line and the branch line to Peterborough.

The station stood originally at the end of what is now a long driveway on the south side of the road.

Regional Road 9 is itself a side trip worth taking, a roller coaster ride through high hills to the west. At least travel as far as Garden Hill 2.5 kilometres west, with its old general store. To continue along the old Midland line return east from Garden Hill, or west from Campbellcroft, to Regional Road 10 and follow it north. The road is scenic, twisting its way through a rugged ridge of hills deposited by the swirling waters of the melting continental glaciers 20,000 years ago. At the first intersection the overgrown right of way crosses from east to west. Six more kilometres brings you to Carmel Corners Road. Although the hamlet itself has vanished, a side trip west for 700 metres will bring you to the right of way where the roadbed and station grounds are barely visible. Glance at the farm north of the road and east of the station grounds, however, to see the old station. Only a cabin-size flag "station," it still sports its railway red paint.

Return to Regional Road 9. Go five kilometres further and you are in Millbrook. Originally a mill town, as the name implies, the original village site was clustered near the mill site on Buster Creek. The railway was built on higher ground one kilometre

C.P.R. Depot, Lindsay, Ont., Canada

The CPR's witch's hat station served the GBS in Lindsay. (TPL)

further west spawning a cluster of houses and hotels there. Lisa Street, on the south side of the main street, marks the site of the busy station grounds. Here the route split, that on the east side of the station leading to Peterborough, that on the west following the main line to Georgian Bay. While a medical centre and new housing now occupy the site, you will still find on the north side of the street the old red brick railway hotel.

From Millbrook the right of way leads northwest across rolling farmlands, after 5.5 kilometres passing under the still active CPR line to Peterborough. It is visible across the field on the south side of Cavan Concession 7/8 which you follow for about five kilometres west of Regional Road 10. This dirt road continues west and then north into the charming village of Bethany. And here the Midland, by then under the ownership of the Grand Trunk Railway, encountered a new rival, the CPR's Georgian Bay and Seaboard line (GBS). Built in 1911 from Port McNicoll to Dranoel, which is "Leonard" spelled backwards, the GBS paralleled the Midland, often within whistling distance of it, to Georgian Bay.

Bethany was born of the Midland, a station village created to serve the railway. When the GBS built its line it ran right beside the Midland through the village. While the small Grand Trunk depot stood beside what is today Highway 7, the two-storey GBS station was a short distance north. Both are now gone. Despite the attractive preserved streetscape of houses and stores, Bethany retains nothing of the community's railway heritage. Stations and tracks are long gone, and even the right of way is now buried beneath Victoria Road 38. And this is the road that you follow, for you are

now tracking not only the Midland Railway but the GBS as well.

Three kilometres north of Bethany, at an intersection, stood a flag station named Brunswick, although even the right of way has all but disappeared. However, just north of this point the road is on the right of way. At the second intersection past Brunswick look for a ghost town named Franklyn. In the early years of this century the narrow dirt road to the east was Franklyn's main street, and contained a church, store, station, and several houses. Amid the new homes are the foundations of these long vanished buildings. A further 1.5 kilometres west of Franklyn the overgrown right of way of the GBS marks the site of the Fleetwood station. There is no evidence of the railway settlement and even the right of way is disappearing on private property.

Return to Franklyn and follow the right of way north into Omemee and Highway 7. The right of way continues north across the highway to what would become its junction with the "missing link." While Peterborough was the original destination of the Midland, Omemee was as close as the main line got. So to fill in the gap, and connect Peterborough with its expanding network, the Midland added the short section east from Omemee to Peterborough, thus completing the "missing link." The site of the junction is just a few blocks north of Highway 7 where a few old buildings linger from those heady days. The building that the GT built to serve as the Omemee station stood a kilometre east, north of the highway. The shack-sized depot was moved to the yard of the school to the west, leaving the asphalt station platform on the west side of the road. A busy highway town now, Omemee contains several old stores and hotels that date from the days of the Midland and the Grand Trunk.

Continue west on Highway 7, a route which leads you past the Midland Railway village of Reaboro. Two kilometres west of Reaboro, Highway 7 bends north at a one-time GBS siding named Hillhead.

The Midland was the first railway to enter Lindsay. Then known simply as the Port Hope and Lindsay, the original track followed the meandering Scugog River along the east side of town and briefly terminated at a station and yard near King Street. As its ambitions grew and the line changed its name to the Port Hope Lindsay and Beaverton, it bridged the river near Pottinger

Street and continued its way west. Then the owners of the Midland decided to venture even further on to Georgian Bay, and renamed it the "Midland." When the Midland merged with Victoria Railway and the WPPL, the need for separate stations ended and a replacement was built at Durham and William. This two-storey building lasted until 1967 when it was demolished.

Although the Midland's main line from Port Hope was abandoned during the 1950s, the "missing link" between Peterborough and Lindsay lasted another three decades. A small section of that right of way is now a walking trail in Peterborough's Jackson Park.

The Midland's "missing link" is now a popular path in Peterborough's Jackson Park.

The GBS entered Lindsay by passing under the Midland near the shore of the Scugog River. Through Lindsay the GBS shared its tracks and station with the CPR's Lindsay, Bobcaygeon and Pontypool branch (see Chapter 14) before continuing westward over a bridge across the river north of the station. Once the railway centre of central Ontario, Lindsay today has not one single metre of active railway track. Although all railway structures and tracks are gone, you can still see the recently abandoned Midland (CNR) right of way along Durham Street in the south end of the town.

From Lindsay to Orillia both old rights of way race each other across the flat farmlands of Victoria County. Follow Highway 7 west of Lindsay to County Road 18 and drive north to Cambray. The Midland's first station west of Lindsay was at Cambray, and it stood about four kilometres southwest of the hamlet on the first concession road west of County Road 18. The right of way has been closed here and a hydro line constructed along it.

The first GBS station west of Lindsay was known as Grasshill. While the station and water tower have long vanished, you can still see the former section foreman's house and the foundation of the tower. A small culvert with the date 1912 crosses a little creek nearby. Although the property is now private, you can drive close enough to see all three. Follow County Road 6 west from Cambray. Watch for where the road bends north. Then, at the five kilometre mark from Cambray, and where the road bends back west, a short dirt road appears on your right. Follow this to the gate which marks the private property. The house is down the lane while the culvert and tower foundation sit beside the road.

West of this point the two lines part company. Continue on County Road 6 to where it bends north and continue west on County Road 9. At Grasshill hamlet, the Midland right of way crosses the road and is marked by the hydro towers that persist along the route. At Woodville you meet County Road 46. Turn north and travel three kilometres to Lorneville. Described in Chapter 4 on the Toronto and Nipissing Railway, this is where the Midland and the T&N crossed. The station with its corner bay window sits in a farm field 100 metres north of the intersection.

The Midland itself is visible as a depression in the embankment on the east side of the highway, and not visible at all on the west. Continue north on County Road 46 to Argyle. Three kilometres north is the right of way for the GBS and the railway station built to serve Eldon, a short distance north. Built by the CPR after that company took over the GBS, the station is now repainted in a bright red and white, and still guards the GBS right of way. Because of its distance from the nearest village, the station, according to the railway's book of station plans, contained living quarters on the second floor. Today it is a house.

Return to Argyle and follow County Road 8 west to Beaverton. This attractive little lakeside town once had two stations. The more recent, demolished in 1992, stood on the still active CNR line which was originally that of the Canadian Northern Railway (CNo). The Midland entered from the east and used a small board and batten station know as Beaverton East. It stood near the corner of Centre and Franklin Streets, the site today of the modern Beaverton Thorah Health Centre. Only the feed service on the west side of the road marks the route of the right of way.

North from Beaverton the CNo and the Midland ran side by side. At Mara Beach, a small community park five kilometres north of Beaverton, the Midland right of way can be seen on the west of the CNR line. The next place to see it is on Mara Concession Road B about 1.5 kilometres west of Gamebridge. A large quarry and an older house mark the location. The GBS, meanwhile, angled straight northwest from Argyle station crossing the Trent River and Canal at "Talbot" where you can still make out the bridge abutments.

From Gamebridge drive north on Highway 12 to Brechin. Here is yet another old CPR station, identical in style to that at Eldon, and again on the right of way. Reincarnated as "Boxcar Willie's" restaurant, the station replicates its original paint scheme and inside displays old CPR posters that once urged onlookers to travel east, west or even overseas using, naturally, the CPR.

The Midland's Brechin station, two kilometres west of the village, is marked today by a railway era house and former hotel. From here the two old lines get back together to run side by side to Uptergrove, a stretch along which, with rival engineers's

The station style used by CP at Eldon on the GBS right of way, and now a house, resembles thousands built by that company across Canada.

find "Ellesmere." While originally the site of a CPR siding (the CPR had intended to make it a major yard), Ellesmere is the labour of love of Cecil Byers, Dave Walmsley and John Smith. Over the years a caboose, a boxcar, the shell of an old steam locomotive, and a working diesel have all been brought in. It is a full-scale backyard railway. Although it only has a few hundred metres of track, it attracts visitors and often plays host to children's birthday parties. The little octagonal Ellesmere "station" never was a railway building. Rather, it was once part of a service station in Atherley. This private museum is at the end of Mara Road 20, south of Highway 12.

For Midland followers this journey ends at Atherley, for here the CNR now takes over to follow the remainder of the route to the town that gave it its name. From the east side of Atherley bridge, the CNR line ventures north to North Bay while west of the bridge, the line was abandoned in 1996.

GBS followers can continue into Orillia where at the foot of the main street, Colborne Street, you can see yet another CPR station, now enlarged and home to the local legion. The structure is brick with a more decorative bay window area, as befits an urban station. The CNR station, a handsome brick structure located at Front and King Streets, postdates the days of the Midland and, restored with Ministry of Transportation funds, remains in use as Chamber of Commerce and a multi-function terminal.

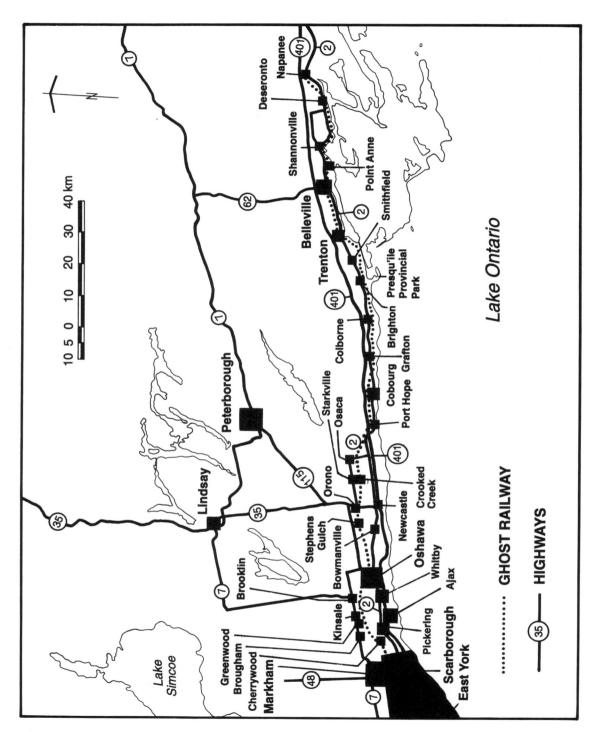

Lake Simcoe

Lake Ontario

40 km
30
20
10
5 0
10 5 0

N

GHOST RAILWAY

HIGHWAYS

35

Napanee
Deseronto
Shannonville
Point Anne
Smithfield
Belleville
Trenton
Presqu'ile Provincial Park
Colborne
Starkville
Osaca
Brighton
Grafton
Cobourg
Port Hope
Orono
Crooked Creek
Newcastle
Stephens Gulch
Bowmanville
Oshawa
Whitby
Ajax
Pickering
Scarborough
East York
Kinsale
Brooklin
Greenwood
Brougham
Cherrywood
Markham

Peterborough
Lindsay

CHAPTER SEVEN

Southern Ontario's Third Main Line:
The Canadian Northern

Backgrounder

In 1895 a railway legend began. In that year partners William MacKenzie and Donald Mann bought a failing Manitoba railway known as the Lake Manitoba Railway and Canal Company, and with it began assembling a network of unused charters and undervalued lines that would soon stretch from coast to coast. But the key link in that network would be the one connecting Toronto and Ottawa. It didn't bother them that two main lines were already destined to run east from Toronto — the 50-year-old Grand Trunk, and that proposed by the CPR

By the time the line was under construction, most of the towns that lined their route were well established. The GT had taken up the best station grounds close to the downtown areas, and had left to the Canadian Northern inferior alignments distant from those towns. That route ventured northeast from Toronto far to the north of places like Oshawa and Bowmanville, and was unable to regain the more desirable lakeshore until Port Hope. From there to

Deseronto the line followed closely that of the GT, the two often running side by side.

Between Napanee and Sydenham, north of Kingston, the CNo incorporated the existing Bay of Quinte (BQ) line (see Chapter 18), but from there laid their own track into Ottawa. From Ottawa the route continued along the south shore of the Ottawa River to Hawkesbury, where it crossed into Quebec sending separate branches to Montreal and Quebec City.

Blind ambition and the construction of yet a third national main line, the Grand Trunk Pacific, however, led to the downfall of the Canadian Northern. The completion of three national main lines, and three east of Toronto that essentially duplicated each other, on the verge of what would be a costly global war, had the makings of financial disaster. When the war ended two lines were bankrupt. To take over the failed lines — the Canadian Northern, the Grand Trunk, and the Intercolonial in the maritimes — and to rationalize the myriad redundant networks, the government created a new company. It was called the Canadian National Railways.

Under the CNR, lines which were once rivals were suddenly redundant. Nowhere was this more evident than east of Toronto. The CNR did not need two lines that ran side by side and served the same communities. So, in 1936 they abandoned the least profitable route, MacKenzie and Mann's Canadian Northern. The line had lasted a mere two decades. Track remained in place in a few areas into the 1940s and a short industrial spur survives yet in Cobourg. Despite the near absence of any effort to preserve the vestiges of this important line, stations, bridges, and railway hamlets nonetheless await the backroading rail fan.

All Aboard

This route begins in Toronto's Leaside community and follows the CNo east to Deseronto.

Every hour of every day, thousands of Toronto motorists on the Don Valley Parkway pass an overgrown flood plain under the Bloor viaduct, unaware that for a few decades these were the railway yards of the Canadian Northern. Similarly, the thousands of residents who enjoy the curving treelined streets of Leaside give little thought that their neighbourhood was once

CNo's Todmorden station stood beneath what is today the Leaside Bridge in Toronto and the point where the CNo branched east from the Grant Trunk. (MTL)

a railway town designed and built by the architects and planners of Mackenzie and Mann.

Leaside today is an upscale residential neighbourhood of East York. Solid two-storey brick houses and attractive bungalows sit beneath tall maples on its curving streets, many such as Hanna named after CNo executives. From the town centre, at Millwood and McCrea, with its park library and small commercial core, the streets radiate outward.

But at least half of Leaside was industrial. East of Laird the railway added factories, several miles of industrial spur lines, and a station. Today the old factories have been replaced by new ones, the CNo yards lie rusting or have been lifted completely. The station still stands with the original engine house across the road and today the squat, red brick structure is the dispatching office for an utility company. You can see it on Esendar Avenue east of Laird.

Meanwhile, down in the Don Valley, the remains of the railway are a little harder to trace. Beside today's CNR track, that's the one on the west side of the valley, and beneath the Leaside bridge, the railway had its Todmorden Station. This two-storey wooden structure marked the point where the CNo ventured northeastward across the river. From the bridge abutments you can follow the roadbed beneath a row of hydro towers east along the valley of Taylor Creek Park. From the east end of the park the TTC subway line runs beside the right of way until, at Warden Avenue, another CNR industrial spur takes over.

Beyond that the right of way angles northeast through Scarborough, largely built upon and scarcely evident except where it defines property boundaries. At Malvern, a one-time farm hamlet situated at the corner of Steeles and Markham in Scarborough, the CNo erected another station, one identical to that at Todmorden. Recent housing developments have wiped all traces of the line and the hamlet, and the station has been gone for years.

From near Malvern the CNo ran neck and neck with the line of CPR, crossing Neilson Avenue on bridges that stood until the early 1990s, and on through the farmlands of Pickering township where, at the community of Cherrywood, both had stations adjacent to each other. While the hamlet of Cherrywood can still be seen at the intersection of Rosebank and the 3rd Concession in Pickering, the stations were on Whites Road one kilometre south of the 3rd Concession. The lines parted company south of the village of Greenwood, where in the Greenwood Conservation area a utility line indicates the CNo right of way.

East of Greenwood, the CNo hugs the foot of the ridge of glacial hills called the Oak Ridges Moraine, passing south of the hamlet of Kinsale. It crosses Highway 12 about 2.3 kilometres south of the village of Brooklin on Highway 7, where the Whitby Port Perry and Lindsay (WPPL) railway had a small station. To avoid confusion, the CNo spelled its station name "Brinlook." A medical clinic now occupies the original station master's dwelling, across from a former bridge abutment.

Nor could the CNo penetrate into Oshawa, settling instead for a station site nearly five kilometres north. Known then as the Oshawa North, the community has been gobbled up by Oshawa's urban expansion and is no longer a distinct community either in name or in appearance. Even traces of the CNo which created the place are hard to pick out. A lane between Taunton and Thissett Streets marks the right of way. The two-storey station, one of several built to an identical pattern between Oshawa and Trenton, survives as a house at 86 Wayne Street, just a few yards from its original location.

The next station was just six kilometres away, and it survives to this day. Continue east on Taunton Road to Solina Road and drive south for two kilometres. You will see it at the end of a long driveway, the former right of way, on the east side of the road. This two-storey station replaced an earlier flag station and saw service on a spur line until the early 1940s.

Once more the line had to keep well to the north of the next major town, Bowmanville. Located 3.5 kilometres away, the railway named the station Tyrone, after a small mill town well to the north. The right of way today passes through a golf course where the station once sat. The location is on Middle Road about four kilometres from the centre of Bowmanville.

Then drive north a short distance to Concession 4 and head east. At Bethesda Road turn north and drive to Stephen Mills Road and the Stephen Gulch Conservation Area. Although there was no station here, this little ghost mill village was the location of a large bridge over Soper Creek. You can see the abutments and a fading photo of the original bridge on the interpretive plaque beside the parking lot.

From Stephen Gulch to Orono, the next station stop, private roads have been constructed on the roadbed. To reach Orono on public roads drive north from the conservation area on Bethesda to Taunton Road and then east to Ochonski Street. Turn south and drive into Orono. This may be the only town that the CNo can call its own, at least on this route. It began life as a mill town on the banks of Orono Creek, but when the railway arrived it received a boost and grew. The main street still retains the appearance it had when the railway was here, with businesses housed in solid brick buildings.

Station Street marks the site of the depot, another structure that copied the design of those at Oshawa and Tyrone. The only railway building still standing at this writing is a wooden warehouse a few blocks east of the main street.

East of Orono the route is no longer visible, having been ploughed under long ago by adjacent farmers. Seven kilometres east the "Starkville" station served the community of Newtonville, some six kilometres south. The building was actually located in a hamlet known as Crooked Creek at the intersection of Newtonville Road. The station grounds were about one kilometre north, and the station itself, now remodelled into a house, was moved north of that.

From Crooked Creek continue east to Regional Road 65. Less than one kilometre before the intersection a dirt road leads north. This was the road to the Osaca station. Nothing remains: the station site is overgrown and the road itself closed to traffic. Osaca is two kilometres north on Regional Road 65 and today is a small collection of houses, a few dating from the days when the Canadian Northern came to town.

The railway entered Port Hope on a high bridge over the Ganaraska River and gave Port Hope its fourth line and its fourth railway station. Of those four sta-

60 GHOST RAILWAYS OF ONTARIO

tions, three survive. The Grand Trunk station, built in 1856 still serves Via passengers; this makes it Canada's oldest station in continuous operation. The Midland Station was located behind Lent's Travel on Walton Street, the main street, while that of the CNo was located on Ontario Street at Howard. Of these, the town's grandest station was the CNo's brick building. With its steep roof lines it was designed by CNo architect Ralph Benjamin Pratt in the Chateauesque style that he had earlier made popular as chief architect for the CPR. It survived the closing of the railway and served as a provincial government building until 1992. Of the four, the only station to be demolished was that of the CPR.

From Port Hope east to Cobourg, a utility line marks the route of the CNo, visible as you travel the short distance between the two communities on Highway 2. Cobourg is worth a visit to see the preserved main street, historic Victoria Hall, the town hall and court, and its lakeside parks.

In Cobourg the CNR and the CPR both cross Ontario Street on bridges. A few metres north of the bridges the CNo crossed. A railway workers' community was squeezed in between the two lines, remaining today an interesting and historic residential area where, along Buchanan Street, a number of traditional railway houses still stand. Cobourg was also the lake port for the abandoned Cobourg and Peterborough

The CNo station in Port Hope was one of the line's grandest, and survives to this day. (MTO)

Railway, the doomed little line that is the subject of Chapter 15.

You can easily see the CNo right of way as it parallels Buchanan Street on the north; and at the west end of Buchanan is the site of the former diamond between the Cobourg and Peterborough and the CNo. A short section of the CNo still serves as an industrial spur line.

While the CPR station was removed in the early 1980s, along with all others along its line, that built by the Grand Trunk still provides passenger service. Via has restored its original high ceiling and its wood trim, and has added traditional wooden benches. The CNo station, however, has long since been removed.

East of Cobourg to Grafton, the telegraph poles still show you the right of way on the south side of Highway 2. From the historic main intersection in Grafton follow Danforth Road south less than two kilometres to a crossroads and a ghost town. (Torontonians shouldn't be too shocked to see Danforth Road in Grafton. The name of two busy streets in Toronto, it was given to the entire route that surveyor Asa Danforth laid out between Toronto and Kingston in 1799. Although much of that pioneer road vanished after the building of the Grand Trunk, portions still appear along the way.) This dirt road marks the CNo right of way and a village that grew up around a cannery. Known as Grafton Station, it consisted of two cannery buildings, a bunkhouse, a few workers' cabins, and the house that you see today. The right of way parallels the lane to the east and is now overgrown. The station, designed like those at Tyrone and Orono, is long gone. A short distance further south both the CNR

and CPR run side by side but have left no railway structures.

Highway 2 between Grafton and Colborne follows one of the more scenic portions of Lake Ontario's shore. Large hills sculpted by glaciers into shapes like the backs of whales force the road to twist and turn. An attractive side trip leads along the Shelter Valley Road north for ten kilometres to Vernonville.

The telegraph poles continue to identify the right of way to the south. New development, including a new arena, makes it almost impossible to trace the CNo through Colborne, although it did angle across the south end of the village. The station, another in the eastern Ontario pattern, sat at the corner of Division and Arthur Streets.

Between Colborne and Brighton the heady days of steam must have presented some strange sights; for here the three main lines all converged and ran side by side into Brighton and beyond. About five kilometres east of Colborne the two remaining lines are immediately beside the highway on the south side.

The railways continued their rivalry through Brighton, a town which boomed when the Grand Trunk located its station there in 1856. That building still stands. The CPR added its track immediately to the south of the GT while the CNo came through along Richardson Street to the north. Unlike other CNo stations on this route, the one in Brighton was much simpler, a single-storey depot with no architectural embellishments. It survived for a number of years as a building on the property of a lumber company. Presqu'ile Point Provincial Park is located nearby and, with its sand dunes and its ancient lighthouse, invites a visit.

Follow Highway 2 east from Brighton. The first road south leads to a point where the CNo ducked under both the GT and the CPR. However, the gap has been filled. From this point the CNo proceeds directly east to Trenton while the CNR and CPR still travel neck and neck northeasterly to the same destination. Four kilometres east, at Smithfield, turn south from Highway 2 onto Lawson Settlement Road and follow Stony Point Road to Power Line Road. This takes you along the right of way for a few metres to English Settlement Road. Turn east. A further four kilometres takes you to Highway 33 on the outskirts of Trenton.

Once the location for three graceful railway stations, Trenton today has none. The Grand Trunk built a large station on its main line three kilometres north of the town at Trenton Junction, the point at which the GT passed over the Central Ontario Railway (see Chapter 7 on the COR). It featured a bell-cast roof and an elevator from the lower tracks. It was replaced in the late 1960s with a shelter. Near the north end of town the CPR added an unusual Elizabethan station, reminiscent of that it clandestinely destroyed in West Toronto in 1982. The one in Trenton came down, more openly, shortly before. In 1909 the CNo took over the COR and its newly constructed three storey station at

The CNo's Trenton station was used by the COR when the CNo added that line to its network. Like all of Trenton's original stations, it was demolished. (MTL)

the corner of Division and Dundas Streets. The station was removed to be replaced by a grocery store.

As you enter Trenton along Highway 33 from the west, you follow the Prince Edward County portion of the old COR. Now abandoned, the route still passes the former roundhouse converted to retail uses. CNo trackage still survives in Trenton in the vicinity of Division Street and on a bridge which crosses the Trent Canal beside the Highway 2 bridge.

There is little point in searching for the line east of Trenton. During the war the Canadian Armed Forces built their extensive Canadian Forces Base Trenton facility here

and obliterated the right of way. Between Trenton and Belleville the CNo swung onto the CPR tracks and shared both tracks and station in Belleville. The CNo station was similar to the brick chateauesque station you saw in Port Hope. But with the demise of the CNo, the building fell into the hands of the CPR which demolished it in the late 1970s.

The best place to resume your pursuit of the CNo is south of Shannonville on Highway 2, 15 kilometres east of Belleville. About one kilometre north of this historic town you can visit the ghost station village of Shannonville Station on the CNR's former GT line. A few houses were built here beside the old stone station to house rail-

The CNo's station at Belleville was, unfortunately, shared with the demolition minded CPR.

way employees. Identical to the other GT stone stations along the line, that in Shannonville was torn down in the early 1970s after sitting empty for a number of years.

To return to the CNo from Shannonville, turn south from Queen Street onto King Street and follow it south for two kilometres to Mohawk Beach. This marks the site of the CNo's Mohawk Station, the depot that served the Tyendinaga Indian Reserve. The road bends here to follow the right of way itself along the shore of the lake, a short but scenic interlude. Along the way look on the east side of the road for the old CNo structure that served as a section foreman's house; it may have also housed the station itself for a while. The road then continues on the right of way for another 1500 metres and then turns sharply east. From this point the right of way itself continues straight ahead as a private driveway.

Drive through the Indian Reserve to Highway 49. Turn south here and travel to Hastings Road 16, which follows the right of way eastward into Deseronto, once the home of the extensive Rathbun lumbering interests which built the Bay of Quinte railway (see Chapter 18). Although Deseronto has a number of interesting historical sights, including the Royal Chapel of the Mohawks and the old town hall, all vestiges of the railway have been removed. Station, track, warehouses, mills — all have been destroyed and replaced with a wide gravel road that parallels the waterfront.

The CNo continued northeast to Ottawa from Deseronto. That portion between Deseronto and Yarker is described in Chapter 18, while much of the remaining portion, from Smiths Falls to Ottawa, remains in use.

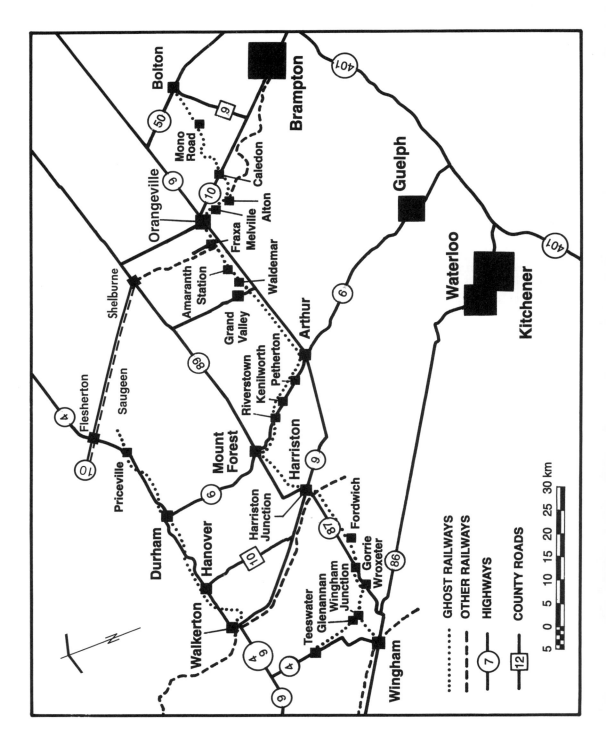

CHAPTER EIGHT

The Toronto Grey and Bruce: A Western Pioneer

Backgrounder

By 1870 the shorelines of Lake Ontario and Lake Erie were the domain of the Grand Trunk, the Great Western, and the dozens of resource railways that led inland from the lake ports.

But a pioneer region far to the northwest of Toronto, known then as the Queen's Bush, was still anybody's territory. Although pioneer farmers had been hewing their rough farms from the bush for nearly twenty years, the railways had yet to arrive.

Among the first on the scene was a direct ancestor of the future CPR, the Toronto Grey and Bruce. Originally conceived as a simple tramway that would lead up the Credit Valley and then along the pioneer Hurontario Street to Collingwood, the proposal was dropped in favour of a more traditional railway. Its first name was the Toronto and Owen Sound Central, but the name soon became the Toronto Grey and Bruce, and construction began in Weston in 1869. By December of 1870 it had reached Bolton and a year later Mount Forest. In 1873 the Grey Extension opened from Orangeville to Owen Sound, while

the Bruce Extension swung westerly from Mount Forest to a terminus at Teeswater. The original plan was to extend the Bruce Extension to Lake Huron by linking with the Wellington Grey and Bruce at Wingham. The WGB rejected the idea, however, and the TGB ended its rails at Teeswater, well inland from the lake. Another 15 years would pass before the TGB finally built a spur line into Wingham.

In 1881 a rival appeared on the scene. The Credit Valley Railway (CVR) had opened its line from Toronto to St. Thomas, with a branch to Fergus and one to Orangeville that paralleled that of the TGB. The following year, the CPR was busy gathering up lines in southern Ontario in preparation for its transcontinental splurge. Among them were the TGB and the Credit Valley. Discovering that it had two railway lines running virtually side by side from Toronto to Orangeville, the CPR dropped the TGB as far as Orangeville. Its trains followed the Credit Valley route to near Orangeville and the TGB route to Owen Sound and Teeswater.

The first stations along the route were, in the words of an early critic, "miserable shanties." Most were single-storey with no architectural embellishments; few had even a bay window. The more important stations, such as those at Mount Forest and Fordwich, were two-storey. Only the structure at Wingham, with a dormer on the second storey and hip gables at the ends, had any aesthetic appeal. After it absorbed the line, the COR replaced the earlier stations with those from their own book of station patterns. These included storey-and-a-half buildings with dormers tucked into sweeping bell cast roofs, or the pleasing little "Swiss Cottage" style used in smaller communities. While most lasted until the late 1960s, only a few remain, non on its original site.

While it abandoned the southern TGB section in 1933, another half century would pass before the CPR removed service from the remaining tracks of the TGB. In 1984 it abandoned its Saugeen to Walkerton branch, and four years later it gave up on its Bruce extension from Orangeville to Teeswater as well as the Fergus branch of the CVR. Only the Grey Extension to Owen Sound remains, its rails disused and rusting.

All Aboard

While this route takes you along the TGB from Bolton to Teeswater, note that the original terminus of the TGB was located roughly beside the Old Fort York in Toronto, near the foot of Bathurst at Front. Known as the Queen's Quay Terminus, the site is now covered over by the abandoned Molson's Brewery, while fill has moved the lake's shoreline south to its present location.

The station designated "South Parkdale" stood on the northeast corner of King and Dufferin Streets.

Bolton is a rapidly growing suburb of Metropolitan Toronto. Save for an unsightly and intrusive parking lot, Bolton's historic commercial core remains visually intact, nestled at the bottom of the steep valley of the Humber River. Because of the valley's depth, TGB railway engineers routed the line above the valley to the south and the west on to Orangeville. In 1908 a "branch" line was opened between Bolton and Sudbury. That "branch" has now become the main line and carries several trains a day. Bolton's first station was situated where the line now passes under Highway 50. But when the Sudbury branch opened in 1908 the COR constructed a new station at the junction three kilometres west. The station survived until 1992.

Between Bolton "junction" and Mono Road to the northwest, the now invisible right of way crosses what is now a commodity for land speculators. Follow Regional Road 9 west from Bolton to the partial ghost town of Sand Hill and turn north on Regional Road 7 to Mono Road, a hamlet that grew around the TGB station. Although the right of way is discernible on the west side of Regional Road 7, a gas station has covered over all evidence on the east side.

The roadbed then makes it way to the rugged Caledon Hills, a roller coaster ridge of sand and gravel left behind by the glaciers 20,000 years ago. To negotiate the hills the railway engineers had to devise a steep horseshoe curve. In 1907 that dangerous bend witnessed one of Canada's deadliest train wrecks. As what some witnesses described that an intoxicated train crew sped into the curve, the train carrying Toronto-bound exhibition excursionists leapt from the tracks. With a roar the boiler exploded as the flimsy coaches flew into each other leaping from the tracks. In the smoldering wreckage seven lay dead, another 114 injured.

The site today is unheralded and forgotten except by local historians and railway enthusiasts. The only sign to mark the place is not an historical plaque but rather a "No Hunting" sign that sits in a gully on the south side of the 10th sideroad, 3.2 kilometres east of Highway 10. You can also see it, from a different vantage, as a driveway to a private residence known as 17202, half a kilometre south of the 10th sideroad on the 3rd Line East.

This sideroad also offers you wide views from the hilly heights of the Mississauga skyline to the south. As you drive north along Highway 10 towards the village of Caledon you will be unable to make out the now redeveloped right of way that angles across the southern part of the village on the west of the highway, although it is a travelled lane on the east. The same holds true for the station. While it still stands near its original location at the end of Toiless Street, renovations have covered its station appearance.

From Caledon you can turn west on Highway 24 to its junction with Highway 136 where you can hike along the Credit Valley Railway's abandoned Fergus branch. Simply drive south into the exclusive residential enclave of Cataract. Just past the popular Horseshoe Inn you will enter a gully where you can park (for a short period of time) and follow a path that leads you to the abandoned line. Here where it climbs the wall of the Credit Valley are some of the most spectacular views that a southern Ontario ghost railway will offer. Here too, where the Fergus branch left the main line, lie the overgrown fields that were once the site of the station, water tower, and the widely known Junction House Hotel.

To continue along the route of the TGB, however, you will need to turn north and take Highway 136 to Alton. This partial ghost town began as a mill town on the rushing waters of the Credit River. Although massive housing developments have swept over its outskirts, you can still visit its historic small downtown, many of its buildings vacant. At the west end of the town is the much livelier "ghost" of the Millcroft Inn, an 1849 woolen mill that is now a popular and elegant hotel and restaurant.

This all sits west of Highway 136. The route itself follows Highway 136 east to cross the rails of the former CVR. However the TGB line is a barely discernible mound about 400 meters south of Highway 136 on the 2nd Line West. This was also the site of a small quarry village and large stone boarding house, which are now on private property and difficult to access.

Melville is still accessible and still alive, although its days as the important crossover of the TGB with the CVR are long past. Drive east from Highway 136 on the 25th sideroad to 1st Line West. As you cross the tracks look south. About 250 metres down, a bend in the line marks the site of the old diamond. This is the point at which the CPR brought the tracks of the CVR and TGB together. From here into Orangeville trains switch onto the former line of the

TGB. That of the CVR, abandoned from this point on, has vanished from the landscape. The handsome red brick house on the northeast corner was once a railway hotel.

In Orangeville the only visible portion of the CVR right of way is at the corner of Townline Road and Orange Street. The short lived CVR station sat on the north side of the main street. The former TGB station, sporting a conical roof dubbed the "witch's hat" style, was removed from its location beside Highway 136 in 1991 and converted to a restaurant. Most of the tracks in the yards have been removed and store only a few freight cars or snowploughs. The only building to survive is the intrigu-

ing two storey maintenance building that in the days of passenger service functioned as the station restaurant. An historic plaque on the north side of the highway tells the tale of the railway.

Although Orangeville has a mixed record in its preservation efforts, the historic main street has been revitalized so that some of the new buildings fit with the architectural texture of the historic townscape. Orangeville is also an opportunity to take a break from your route in the sit-down restaurants or fast food eateries.

To follow the next segment of the TGB, the more recently abandoned Bruce Extension to Teeswater, take Highway 9 west from Orangeville.

Doctors arrive at the scene of the Horseshoe Wreck, too late to save many.   (OA)

About seven kilometres west of downtown Orangeville, Amaranth Line 3 leads north for one kilometre to the former junction of the Owen Sound and Teeswater branches of the TGB. Today only the Owen Sound branch survives. On the west side of the road you can see the line bending north and the remains of the Teeswater branch wending its lonely way west. In the arm of the "Y" an attractive station stood until the late 1960s. However, the location never gave rise to any sizeable settlement. A few new industries have settled in the area.

Six kilometres further west County Road 6 leads to Waldemar, the next TGB station stop. Amid the overwhelming wave of new housing developments, you will encounter the old Presbyterian church and the village store, the only reminders of Waldemar's beginnings as a mill village on Willow Brook. Turn right onto Station Street, cross the bridge over the brook, and drive one half kilometre to the site of the station. Although the track ran along the north side of the street, if you look carefully behind a small white house on the south side, you can yet see the wonderfully preserved form of the tiny Waldemar station, the only example of the "Swiss Cottage" style to survive on the line. From the north side of the bridge you will see the abutments of the railway bridge.

The next station, also preserved, stood only 2.5 kilometres west at Grand Valley. Much larger than Waldemar, the village still retains its 19th century main street; however, in May of 1985 a devastating tornado darkened the skies and roared through town, blowing to pieces many of its grand turn-of-the-century homes.

The right of way crosses Highway 25 at the speed limit sign on the south end of town. As you approach you can see on a knoll about 250 metres to the west the former station, an attractive early style that incorporated a second floor gable into its steep bell-cast roof line. Today it is a short distance from its original location and survives, little altered except for new siding, as a house.

Arthur, 12 kilometres further west on Highway 9, began life in the 1850s as an important stopping place at the intersection of two important pioneer settlement roads. As the flat and fertile farmlands around it filled, Arthur grew slowly. Then, in 1872, the TGB line passed to the north of the fledgling settlement and Arthur suddenly boomed. Grain and lumber were shipped out on the frequent trains as businesses and factories gathered at trackside.

Its historic main street lies along Highway 6 north of Highway 9. From this main street you can drive to the station grounds by turning north at the stop light and proceeding one kilometre to the recreational grounds. While the playing fields have covered over the right of way on the west side of the road, you can yet make out the site of the station and the sidings on the east. The station has been moved and converted to a house, its style identical to that in Grand Valley.

Highway 6 takes you through a trio of tiny settlements to Mount Forest. The first of these, about 5.5 kilometres from the traffic light in Arthur, is Petherton. The three little houses are all that survive of what was once a larger stopping place on the Garafraxa Road. It was too close to Arthur to boom with the railway; although the timetables list nothing for this location, the village may have had a siding. Today it is a virtual ghost town.

Another five kilometres leads to Kenilworth. A "road" town from pioneer days, it grew with the arrival of the railway and still contains a store, bank, and post office. The former station grounds, a few metres east of the main crossroads, retain no vestige of the railway days. Overgrown and unused, the site bears no evidence of the sidings, station grounds or any of the other railway buildings that served the community.

About five kilometres north of Kenilworth, a bridge soars above the landscape carrying traffic over a rail line that is no more, and a village that is no more. Never more than a stopping place on the Sydenham Road, Riverstown has no buildings linked to the pioneer or railway era. A

number of newer country homes create more a suburban than an historic atmosphere.

For the next couple of kilometres you can view the right of way as a mound on the west side of the highway. It was sold to adjacent owners and has no distinctive use.

Despite its prosperity as a country service town, Mount Forest has lost all vestiges of its considerable railway heritage. Once proposed as the terminus for the TGB, Mount Forest also saw the WGB's Durham branch pass through town, but today you will find neither. Tracks, stations, and rights of way have all gone, smothered by new development — a truck storage yard here, apartments there — and forgotten. When the

Near the site of the TGB station in Wingham, you can still find the peculiar looking WGB station.

TGB chose Teeswater as its terminus over Mount Forest, the main line was re-routed westward on the south bank of the Saugeen River, leaving only a kilometre-long spur line into town.

Take Highway 89 west from Mount Forest to Wellington County Road 6 and follow it south to Minto Concession Road 10-11 and turn west. The right of way, used here as a snowmobile trail, parallels the road on the north side. Rejoin Highway 89, turn south, and drive into Harriston, an important early mill town. After starting out as a stopping place on the Sydenham settlement road, Harriston boomed when two railways roared into town within just a few years of each other. To find the TGB station grounds, turn north onto Elora Street, Highway 9, and drive to Louise. This overgrown area shows no sign of station, sidings, or any other railway building. The only railway age building is the Speers Seed factory, located a block west of the highway and close to the point where the TGB crossed the Owen Sound branch of the WGB.

Highway 87 west from the main intersection not only leads you back to the TGB right of way, but on its way passes one of the more delightful preserved stations in western Ontario. Three blocks west of the main street and now a seniors' drop-in centre, the building displays the GT's western Ontario style. Found also in Hanover (where it still survives) and Walkerton (where it was demolished) it exhibits a hexagonal bay window and a varied roof line. A tower over the street entrance was removed many years ago.

Highway 87 parallels the TGB to a trio of Huron County villages: Wroxeter, Gorrie, and Fordwich. All are mill towns, all are within just a few miles of each other, all prospered then stagnated, and since then, in many respects, time has stood still.

Fordwich, 12 kilometres west of Harriston, failed to prosper to the extent that Wroxeter and Gorrie did, but by 1860 it could claim a mill, hotel, and church. Although the arrival of the TGB did add a feed mill and shipping yards, it did not bring the boom that many other towns enjoyed. Turn south onto County Road 30 and enter town on Patrick Street. You will cross what is clearly the right of way on the northern outskirts of the village, but nothing survives of the days of rail. Both stations, the original two-storey TGB and its smaller successor CPR station, have been moved to new locations, one to become a house, the other a farm out-building. While County Road 30 veers to the right upon entering the core of the village, the historic main street angles toward the left. On this old street you can still see some of the former stores and hotels, now closed or converted to residences, that once made Fordwich a busy place. West of Fordwich, as far as the Maitland River, a snowmobile path follows the right of way.

Gorrie lies only ten kilometres west of Fordwich and was yet another Maitland River mill town. Within five years of its founding in 1854, Gorrie had boomed to a population of 400 and enjoyed three hotels, two sawmills, a steam mill, and a cheese factory. The arrival of the TGB had little effect on the place and it did not achieve "village" status until 1895. Still, it has fared better than Fordwich, and still has a handful of stores doing business on its main street. While its mill town heritage is celebrated with a riverside park and a preserved wooden mill, its railway heritage has left little trace. The right of way, which lies along the highway at the northern limits of the village between Williams Street and the highway, is simply vacant land; Hunts Lumber company, on the right of way, is the only link to its railway heritage.

The third in this trio of mill towns is Wroxeter. Of the three it experienced both the greatest boom and bust. Even before the TGB had reached this far, Wroxeter had three hotels and several industries along the river. Indeed, the first station was not in Wroxeter but rather halfway between Wroxeter and Gorrie. Later, a station was built on the northern fringes of the village and attracted a small cluster of houses and stores. But the arrival of the automotive age treated Wroxeter the most harshly of the three and its population plunged from a high of 700 in 1900 to less than 300 in 1960. On its way down it lost its status as an incorporated town. When I described Wroxeter in a ghost town book published a decade ago as a partial "ghost town," 15 of its 18 stores sat abandoned. Since then, many have been removed while others sport new occupants including a restaurant named after a cartoon ghost, Casper.

In Durham, on the Walkerton branch, the TGB bridge has been declared a heritage structure and redecked to permit pedestrians.

More evidence of Wroxeter's revitalization is a riverside development grandly called Wroxeter "Harbour." But despite this new life, Wroxeter's railway days are gone. While the main part of the town lies south of the highway, the station grounds were to the north a few metres along Lawrie Street. But you wouldn't know it: although a few older structures, including a store that now sells antiques, mark the general location, no railway buildings survive; The right of way lingers as a recreational trail that is used by equestrians as well as by hikers and snowmobilers.

TGB engineers heading west out of Wroxeter had now to decide whether to branch south to Wingham or north to Teeswater, the TGB terminus. Ten kilometres north on County Road 12, you will turn onto Turnberry Concession Road 10-11 and drive six kilometres west to a location maps label Glenanan; the train men knew it as Wingham Junction. Here, in what is now the middle of a pasture, they would switch either north to the line's end, or south to Wingham. A pair of yellow brick houses, one with the station name board, mark the site of this once important railway point.

In the north end of Wingham, east on North Street beside Martha Street, a string of older houses marks the location of the CPR's station. The right of way, however, is a mound, barely visible and overgrown. Further south on the main street another kilometre will bring you again to the WGB and another of its intriguing old GT stations. Its twin towers and main street entrance give it a style unique among western Ontario stations. At the time of writing, however, it was boarded up and for sale.

Wingham was laid out as a government town plot for pioneer settlers and grew slowly until the arrival of the Kincardine branch of the WGB in 1872. After being rebuffed by the WGB in its bid to link with that line, the TGB succeeded in avoiding Wingham for another 15 years, choosing Teeswater as its terminus instead. Even when the link was added it did not connect directly with the WGB. Located 14 kilometres north of Wingham on Highway 4, Teeswater was the terminus for nearly a century, with the station, yards, and engine house. Except for a yellow brick former hotel on the west side of the road, and a Co-op gas bar which occupies the station site and the right of way itself on the east side of the road, all at the southern limits of the village, nothing remains to relive that role.

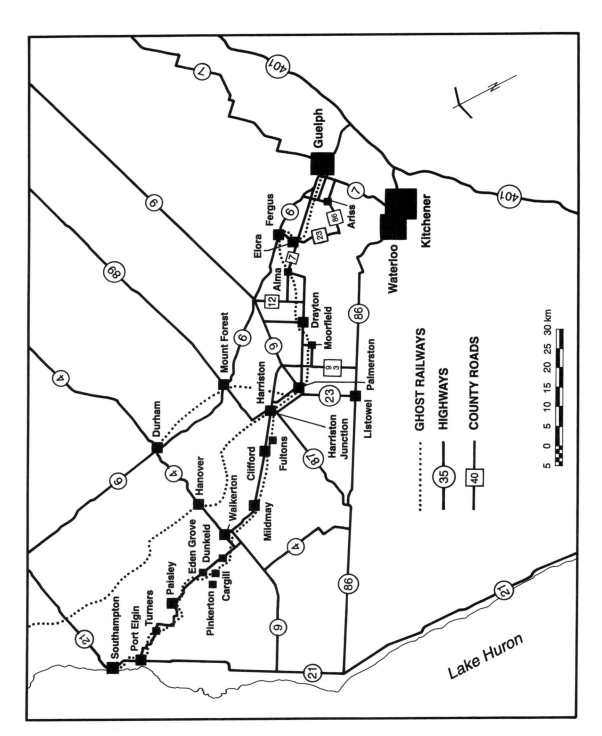

CHAPTER NINE

The Wellington Grey and Bruce: The Bluewater Line

Backgrounder

Ontario's early railway builders raced each other to Lake Huron and the valuable trade that would funnel through its ports. The Northern Railway with its route to Collingwood was the first; the Hamilton and Northwestern, also to Collingwood, the Brantford and Lake Huron and the Guelph and Goderich, both to Goderich, and the Toronto Grey and Bruce to Owen Sound, all followed in short order. And there was the Wellington Grey and Bruce.

It started out calling itself the Canada Northwest, and in 1856 projected a route from Southampton, on Lake Huron, to Toronto. But by the time construction was finished in 1872, the line was much shorter, linking only Guelph with Southampton, with branches to Owen Sound, Kincardine and Durham. Then, during the great railway expansion of the wars of the 1880s, the WGB was gobbled up by the Grand Trunk.

Most of the towns that lined the route are small, its factories and industries family run. It was, as it still is, the heart of Ontario's farm country. Rolling pastures are dotted with solid barns and handsome farm homes of yellow brick or stone, farms that were key to the WGB's profits. Much of its business came from shipping crops and cattle, or from the grain elevators that seemed to loom above every station.

But as highways improved and trucks moved in, as industries moved to larger cities, the WGB (by this time the CNR) lost traffic. By 1984, only the branch to Owen Sound remained, with a connection southward to Palmerston to Stratford along the former Stratford and Huron route. In 1995, the Stratford to Owen Sound section was abandoned, leaving a once-serviced western Ontario with no trackage at all north of Goderich.

One of the key reasons for CNR's massive branch line abandonment program lies with antiquated railway labour contracts. Such contracts keep employees in stated job categories regardless of how little work there is, and this inflexibility made the short branch lines uneconomical to operate. Short line companies, however, operate without union contracts and use employees to the fullest by assigning them a variety of tasks.

The end result? The line is lifted and the jobs are lost.

All Aboard

This route takes you along the old main line from Guelph to Southampton. From Guelph the line makes its way northwestward to Palmerston, once the smoky hub of the WGB's several spokes. From Palmerston it then continues northwesterly to Walkerton and then to Southampton and the blue waters of Lake Huron.

This is old Ontario farm country: sturdy mill towns, many of them already busy when the railway arrived, and family farms form the backbone of the area. Country pragmatism has little room for nostalgia, however, and only a few vestiges of the area's railway heritage have been preserved. Many are still there simply because abandonment, being so recent, has not disposed of everything yet.

Palmerston residents bring to life the abandoned WGB divisional yards with their annual handcar races. But CN has other plans.

The original WGB stations were simple and unadorned. Board and batten structures, they sported no gables or other architectural embellishments. But when the Grand Trunk began to replace them after 1882, they dipped into their pattern book and came up with octagonal bays, hip dormers, and eclectic rooflines. The station at Chesley was even crowned with one of those unusual witch's hat roofs. While a few of the GT depots have managed to cling to life (the last one in Chesley, sadly, did not), the last of the WGBs, in Hanover, was demolished in the 1990s, after serving as a storage shed.

Before starting this route, it's worth looking at Guelph's Grand Trunk station on Garden Street. You can then follow the WGB from its former junction with the GT on Alma Street, north along Edinburgh Road. Here it still serves an an industrial branch with spur lines leading to the many factories in northwest Guelph. Edinburgh Road ends at Highway 7. Turn west to Silvercreek Parkway and drive north. From a T intersection at County Road 51 drive east to County Road 7, the Garafraxa Road. Predating the railway era by three decades, this road was constructed to entice pioneer settlers northwestward to a dark and foreboding wilderness then known as the "Queen's Bush." Early villages or "stopping places" with their hotels and general stores appeared at frequent intervals along the route.

After driving three kilometres north on County Road 7 you pass one of those old pioneer hotels at Ponsonby. While most of what used to be Ponsonby has vanished, the hotel still sits on the west side of the road and is today a house. The WGB parallels the road, but because it is located along the back of farm properties, it is difficult to follow closely. About six kilometres from Ponsonby you cross the WGB at the south end of Elora. The station stood on the east side of the road. An original WGB, it was built in 1870 and survived until 1969. Simple in its appearance, it was a wide building with a shallow sloping roof; it lacked any ornamentation, even a bay window for the operator.

Despite losing its station, Elora has managed to save much of its heritage, largely because it makes so much money. Attracted partly by the steep limestone walls of the Elora Gorge, visitors may also stay in the magnificent old stone Elora Mill Inn, or visit the many interesting shops on the narrow side streets.

From Elora the line swung east to Fergus. The site of WGB ground-breaking, Fergus had an identical depot to Elora's. When it burnt down in 1902, the GT replaced it with a beautiful towered station, much like the one which stood in Grimsby. In 1982, because it was no longer useful to them, the CNR demolished it. Less than a block away stood the CPR's former Credit Valley Railway station near George and Breadalbane Streets. With the tracks and stations of both railways gone, the only evidence of any railway activity here is the former railway hotel, a handsome stone structure that still stands on George Street.

From Fergus the WGB swung back westward and angled across Wellington County's farmlands, but your route leads back through Elora and north again on the Garafraxa Road, County Road 7. A little over three kilometres from the Elora suburb of Salem, the now abandoned right of way crosses the road where the station site for Alma is now utterly barren. Alma itself, once a crossroads farm hamlet, has boomed into a dormitory town for Guelph.

In Alma turn left onto County Road 17 and drive southwest for 3.5 kilometres to County Road 8 and then turn northwest. Six kilometres takes you to Drayton, a former mill town which boomed when the rails arrived and has boomed again as yet another commuter town for Guelph. The railway line stayed away from the centre of town and crossed one kilometre to the northeast. To reach the site, turn right at the main intersection, cross the river, and drive to the top of the hill. Here among the many newer homes stand two rail-age yellow-brick houses and the Nieuwland feed mill. This was the location of Drayton's simple wooden depot.

Return to the main intersection and drive west out of Drayton for six kilometres and turn south toward Moorefield, a gritty little farm town. The station stood at the north end of the small line of stores. However, much of the old right of way has been built over and little of the railway remains. From Moorefield drive west on Maryborough Concession Road 8. The right of way parallels the road and remains open. At Wellington County Road 9, turn right and follow it for just over two kilometres, then turn left onto Perth County Road 2 and drive five kilometres to Palmerston.

A contrast in bridges pits the tiny bridge over a farm road against the mighty trestle over the Saugeen River in Paisley.

At the time of writing Palmerston remains a rail lover's treasure trove. Once the hub of the WGB, it contained extensive divisional yards. Different branches radiated outward like spokes from a wheel. To the southeast was the main line from Guelph; to the southwest was the Listowel branch. While the main line continued northwest, the Durham branch led northeast. They are all abandoned now, rusting and overgrown. The large two-storey wooden station sits empty, its windows boarded and its red paint fading. Hovering above the yards is Palmerston's landmark, a wrought iron foot bridge that stretches 250 metres over the once busy railway yards. While the Listowel branch which enters from the west still has rail, the once busy main line south to Guelph ends in a stub beside King Street.

In a small park beside the station an historic plaque commemorates the founding of Palmerston, while at the north end of the yard, steam engine number 81 sits silent. Let us hope that more than the solitary steam engine and a fading mural of a steam train that asks you to "Stop and shop in Palmerston" will survive to celebrate this town's remarkable railway heritage.

Some residents are doing their part. Each spring, rail fans and fun seekers alike gather here for the annual Palmerston Handcar Races. Using a handcar specially designed and manufactured by Bell's Welding and Hal South Manufacturing, contestants compete for the best time over a 300-metre section of track. Thus, for a few hours every year, Palmerston is a rail centre again.

The continuation of this living heritage depends upon cooperation from both the CNR and government. Past experiences with both sources, however, have not been encouraging.

From the crossing on Palmerston's main street drive east on Highway 23 to County Road 9 and turn north. Two kilometres north at Minto Concession 2/3 the Durham branch crosses the road. The right of way, here with track still down, at the time of writing at least, follows you to Highway 9 and then west into Harriston. At the traffic lights in Harriston turn south onto Highway 87 and drive three blocks to the crossing. The station that greets you here, still well preserved, is typical of the solid, yet elaborate design that the GT added on this line. Today it is preserved as a seniors' drop-in facility. Two blocks northwest of the station is Harriston Junction. Not only does the Owen Sound extension branch north from the main line at this point, but the TGB crosses it at right angles as well. While the Owen Sound branch still has its track (although not likely for long) the old main line to Southampton sits abandoned.

Follow Highway 9 west for 7.5 kilometres to Minto Sideroad 7 and turn south one half kilometre. This was known as Fulton's Station, and trains would stop at a siding and small shed-sized flag station. Nothing survives at this location aside from a pair of farms. Continue along Highway 9 into Clifford. The main street, where handsome main street businesses once stood, has lost much of its 19th century warmth and decor to newer buildings with little character. One half kilometre south of the highway, from the lights at the intersection, the station grounds also lie barren, with nothing but a yellow house, the former station hotel, to recount the WGB. The station was a board and batten depot typical of the style that the WGB put everywhere, but it has been gone for years.

Mildmay is a welcome contrast. Much of its main street, lined with 19th century stores of yellow brick, remains intact. St. Paul's United Church, built of wood and crowned with a large octagonal steeple, and Sacred Heart Roman Catholic church, neighbours on Peter Street just a block west of the main street, represent spectacular examples of early Ontario church architecture.

There is even some heritage to see at the site of the old station. Drive one half kilometre south of the main intersection to the trackless railway crossing. Although the WGB station was demolished in 1971, you will find the Station Tavern. Proudly proclaiming its railway heritage as the hostelry that served train passengers, the tavern also boasts a green and black CNR passenger coach. Completing this railway landscape is an old railside industry, the John Hauser turnip produce factory.

For two kilometres north from Mildmay the railway line hugs the west shoulder of Highway 9, with a small wooden trestle still in place at the one kilometre mark. Six kilometres from Mildmay, the road and railway both enter Walkerton. The administrative town for Bruce County, and a bustling milling centre, Walkerton was well established before the railway arrived. To avoid both high urban land costs and the steep valley

Because it marked the end of the line, the WGB architects put more flourish into the design of the Southampton station. It is now a restaurant.

of the Saugeen River, the railway builders located the station nearly two kilometres from the centre of town. To find this location stay on Highway 9 as it bends west, joining Highway 4 in the process. After less than one kilometre you will cross the right of way. A short distance to the north the former freight shed, weathered and sagging, is still barely standing, and beyond that is the yellow aluminum shed that replaced the Grand Trunk station. The GT depot, which survived into the 1960s, resembled that at Harriston.

To visit the centre of town, follow McGivern Street north from the "station" to Jackson Street and turn right. On Jackson you will pass the 19th century stone jail, still in service, and the former town hall which now serves as a theatre. Durham Street, the main street, is utilitarian with many businesses still housed in turn-of-the-century buildings. But for a different example of early industrial architecture, turn north onto Colborne from Durham. At Catharine Street, Georgian College has placed its facilities in the 1902 Walkerton Ginger Wine Company factory.

Leave Walkerton by driving west on Durham Street up out of the valley of the Saugeen River for four kilometres to Bruce County Road 3 and turn north. The next string of towns on this route are treasures from the past — hardy little farming towns, many features of which remain little changed from those bustling days of rail. As you proceed north, a large stone building looms on the crest of a gentle hill. A long established landmark, it is the Dunkeld Tavern and the only building in "town." This two-storey stone pioneer hostelry with the name on the roof is the only survivor of a small crossroads hamlet that catered to set-

tlers bound for the north to clear the forested lands of northern Bruce County. The track ran about one kilometre west, a location marked only by a siding.

The next community is Cargill, with many handsome late 19th century houses and commercial buildings. Turn west on County Road 32 and look along the small main street to see the now closed Baillie factory, the Royal Bank in an old brick structure, a trio of general stores, and a large hotel now converted into apartments. But the main prize in this town of prizes is the old mill. Now owned by Howson and Howson, it sports an architectural feature rare among Ontario mills: a mansard roof.

Continue straight north from Cargill to the next pair of small settlements, Pinkerton and its station village, Eden Grove. While no settlement existed at Cargill's station grounds, a small community grew around those at Pinkerton. The old mill village itself still contains a few rustic vestiges of its pioneer days, although functionally it is almost a ghost town.

Return east to County Road 3 and resume your northward course. One kilometre from Eden Grove look to the east. Sitting in isolation, near the road, is the house that once was the Cargill station. Different from the patterns that the GT erected south of Walkerton, its distinguishing feature is the octagonal gable above the bay window. Aside from new siding, the structure has changed little in appearance from the times when steam engines, puffing black coal smoke, would hiss to a halt before it.

The right of way closes in on the road for the eight kilometres to Paisley, much of it now used by snowmobilers. Notice the "stop" signs where the roadbed crosses the county roads. The right of way crosses back to the west and as it does so it passes the site of the Paisley station grounds. The depot here was an original simple WGB model which the Grand Trunk never replaced; it was demolished in the 1960s.

Paisley is another treasure trove of historic delights, both railway and pioneer. Local history enthusiasts have preserved a number of pioneer buildings — the town hall with its cupola, the wooden sawmill and the grist mill that was among the last in Ontario to be powered by water, and even an old wooden fire hall. By following Inkerman Street west from the main street, you come to the giant trestle that the WGB built to cross the Saugeen River. Looming nearly forty metres over the swirling waters, it requires three concrete supports and considerable wooden trusses at either end to support it. But given the recent abandonment of the line one wonders how much time will pass before it too is removed.

Drive north through Paisley to Bruce Road 11 and turn west. Follow it for almost seven kilometres and turn north onto an unmarked gravel road. Check the height of your vehicle for the road passes beneath a tiny trestle that is a mere 3.4 metres above the roadway (one wonders again for how much longer). Continue for another four kilometres to a stop sign and turn west. A few metres from here the right of way crosses the road at what was called Turner's. Here the station was little more than a shack situated beside the section foreman's dwelling. Both are gone and the only evidence of the vanished community is a former general store, now used as a private home.

The abandoned railway continues to follow the crest of the Saugeen River valley and all the way to Port Elgin. Your route takes you west past Turner's for another three kilometres where you turn north onto another unmarked road. As the road bends west look for Saugeen Sideroad 17 and turn north. This riverside drive takes you to another stop sign where you turn left and hug the rim of the Saugeen River valley into Port Elgin.

Drive to the main street and turn north. Now a popular Lake Huron resort community, Port Elgin has prospered since the demise of the railway. To reach the station grounds turn right onto Market Street, which is disappointing in that nothing remains to mark the heritage of the railway. The station was another of those simple WGB board and batten structures that lasted until the 1960s and then was demolished. But for a scenic diversion follow Market Street back west and go right to the lake. Here, North Shore Park, complete with its own miniature railway, offers bathing and picnicking facilities.

Follow the lakeshore drive, a surprisingly scenic lakeside route, for the six-kilometre drive to Southampton, the terminus of the line and of your journey. (The right of way, however, is closer to Highway 21 and indeed hugs it closely as it enters town. The roadbed is now popular with snowmobilers.)

When you reach Morpeth Street in town turn west from Highway 21 to Grosvenor. Having survived the demise of the railway, the Southampton station today attracts restaurant-goers in its new guise as "Trax" restaurant. The GT's architects put extra effort into the appearance of the street side of the station, adding a gabled roof and covered entrance way. The high gable over the bay window on the track side is characteristic of those used on other GT stations along the WGB. Southampton's short main street leads down to a lakeside garden and public beach. From here you can see the historic Chantry Island lighthouse, one of a series given the name of Imperial Tower as a result of its slender majestic lines. Cabins and motels offer plenty of opportunity for overnighting.

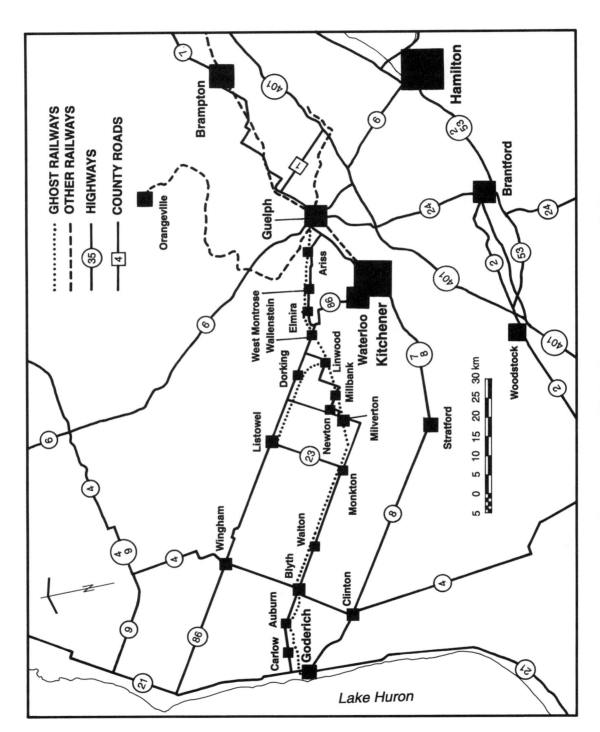

CHAPTER TEN

The Guelph and Goderich: A Link to the Lake

Backgrounder

Relative to the railway development of western Ontario, the Guelph and Goderich (G&G) was a latecomer. Although plans existed as early as the 1870s to link Guelph with Lake Huron, the depression of the 1890s delayed any progress until after the turn of the century. Pushed by the city of Guelph, which was anxious for its third railway line (in its early years it already had connections on the Great Western and Grand Trunk), the line was at last completed to Goderich in 1907. From Guelph south to a little railway village named Guelph Junction, the city of Guelph owned what was then called the Guelph Junction Railway, built as a link between the G&G and the Credit Valley Railway. All were ultimately swallowed by the CPR.

Passing through some of Canada's best farmland, the line ran straight and flat. Only three bridges of any size were needed: that over the Grand River, and two across the Maitland. The towns and villages along the route had already been established by this time, and the arrival of the G&G had only a marginal impact upon their economy or their townscapes. From its book of sta-tion patterns, however, the CPR brought to the towns on the line some of its handsomest depots.

All Aboard

This is a journey that leads you through old Ontario. Farm towns, prosperous and pragmatic, have retained traditions and businesses that have operated for a century: feed mills, general stores, and hotels. In many, the only thing missing is the station. You will still see some of Ontario's most attractive and elegantly preserved stations, a pair of which are still in railway use.

Much of your route takes you through Mennonite country, an area which, with its horse-drawn buggies, still has the look, sound, and smell of another time. Here members of traditional Mennonite groups shun cars and electricity and cling to lifestyles that only our grandparents would remember. Horses drawing buggies and ploughs are everywhere, clip-clopping along the streets of Elmira or Linwood, or loping gracefully through a wide field.

Begin this trip at a real live station in downtown Guelph. The old Grand Trunk station, with its tower over the entrance, still sees four Via trains a day and has been designated by Parks Canada's Historic Sites Branch as a heritage station. On the other hand, the CPR station on the Guelph and Goderich route met a peculiar fate. In an effort to save it, a local group disassembled it brick by brick and removed it to a new site for reassembly. However, no one seems to remember how it originally was put together, and the bricks sit to this day by a waiting foundation on the outskirts of Galt.

Near the Via station, on Garden Street, situated ironically behind the bus depot, sits old steam engine 6167. East of the display,

the G&G line passes under a wide bridge that carries the CNR tracks and, of course, the few Via trains that the government has allowed to continue.

At the bridge turn north onto Woolwich Street. The line, which still has tracks here to serve industries in the north end of Guelph, passes Goldie Mill Park at the corner of Cardigan and Norwich Streets, a block east of Woolwich. Here an old stone mill, and a siding, have become the centrepiece of a small park. When you reach Highway 7 turn west to Silvercreek Parkway and turn north. As you cross the right of way you will see that from this point on it is abandoned. For now hikers use it as a pleasant retreat while railway and govern-

The Guelph and Goderich right of way crosses some of Ontario's richest farmlands. Here it once bridged the Grand River.

ment bureaucrats decide upon its disposition. Continue north to County Road 30 and follow it west to County Road 86 which takes you north to Ariss.

The gravelled right of way here skirts the highway on the north side and is popular with all terrain vehicles and snowmobiles. Turn right at the general store. Although most of this one-time farmers' village and station stop now consists of modern backsplits, you will find at the end of this side street two older houses that were built when the line came through. To the west of the store, the small yellow house is the former station, now unrecognizable.

Continue west on County Road 86 to Regional Road 23 and drive north 700 metres. This brings you to a bridge over the right of way with a wide view to the west. In the distance you can still see the abutments and supports of the bridge that spanned the swirling Grand River. If you travel south on Regional Road 23 from County Road 86 you will come to a bridge of a different kind, in fact the only one of its kind: Ontario's last covered bridge. Built in 1881 as one of five such structures in the province, the West Montrose covered bridge has been restored and still resounds with hoofbeats as Mennonites urge their horse-drawn wagons through.

West Montrose had a station as well. The site lies north of County Road 86 on Woolich Road 62. Although nothing remains at the site, the building was moved a short distance west to serve as a farm outbuilding. Shed-like in design (it didn't even have a peaked roof), it retains its red paint and its orange and blue name board.

What has become Regional Road 86 at the Waterloo Region boundary, continues into Elmira, the heart of Mennonite country. The station grounds and right of way, north of the road on Arthur Street, have been sold to Martin Mills retail store and Electronix, and no evidence of the days of rail remain. Nevertheless, downtown Elmira offers a worthwhile pause. Many old stores, including the Coach House on the corner, remain in use, beside them new sidewalks of red brick and the street lights with period lamps. The Old Town Village is a modern shopping centre designed to blend unobtrusively with the historic town streetscape, and it reflects an old world atmosphere topped off with a parking area for Mennonite buggies.

Wallenstein, the next station stop on the railway, sits about ten kilometres west of Elmira. Although nothing of note remains at the site of the station grounds north of the main intersection, a feed mill still survives on the route. West of the hamlet, still on Regional Road 86, you cross the Conestogo River where you can see the bridge abutments of the railway line. At both Elmira and Wallenstein the station was a storey-and-a-half CPR wooden depot, labelled as "Station Plan # 10" in the CPR planbook, with an attached freight shed and a small dormer tucked into the sweeping bell-cast roofs. Neither survived the 1960s.

Regional Road 6 leads south from what has become Highway 86 to Linwood, a busy Mennonite town. Members of the black-garbed sect shop here in stores that resemble shops of a hundred years ago. Even a refreshing pause in the Linwood pub may reveal another country tradition popular with some of the Mennonite men folk. In Linwood, the right of way cuts a wide swath across William Street which runs north of the main intersection. The freight sheds are visible on the north side of the vacant station grounds on the east side of the street. Beyond the sheds a two-storey house with a suspiciously familiar railway-like bay window is the reconstructed Linwood station. West of the intersection the junction between the Listowel branch and the main line has been abandoned for so long that it is invisible. The main line right of way is clear, however, having been abandoned only in 1991; south of the road it displays a stop sign for snowmobilers.

From the G&G main line take a short side trip along the Listowel branch. The only items of note along this branch, since it has been gone for so long, are the old right of way still visible from Wellington Street, south of the main street in Listowel, and the former Dorking station, still on its original site one half kilometre south of the Dorking general store on Highway 86. Although the lower portion has been altered, the two-storey shape of the old station is still evident. The trademark hip dormer identifies it as a CPR western plan station known as "Type 12." The G&G's Listowel station, a single-storey brick structure with intricate patterns in the red and yellow brick, survived the demise of the railway and was used as a Hydro office until the late 1980s. It is now gone.

Let's return now to the main line.

Drive west of Linwood on Regional Road 17 until you reach Wellesley Town-

The GG's branch line station in Listowel survived as a hydro office until the 1980s, when it was demolished.

ship Road 16 and turn south. You will see stop signs on the right of way for the more recent form of locomotion, snowmobiles. Turn west on Wellesley Road 9, cross the right of way again, and then travel south on Wellesley Road 20. You soon reach Perth County Road 6 which leads west to Milbank. The station grounds are north on County Road 7, where you can still find old foundations of a warehouse and the vacant station grounds, both behind the school at the corner of these two roads.

From the school, follow Waterloo Street and drive to Main Street to see the centre of this old-time country village. The Zehr's country store, the former hotel, and the feed mill, all older structures, and often with a horse-drawn wagon parked in front, evoke an image that has changed little in a century. This is living history.

As you continue west on County Road 6 look on the west side of Stratford Street for two sets of bridge abutments over the Nith River. That closest to you is the old road, the other the railway bridge. Protocol that dictates how rail lines are disposed of allows the municipality the option to purchase the right of way. If the municipality refuses, the route is offered to the abutting owners. Unlike in Wellesley township where the right of way is a snowmobile trail, here in Mornington township ditches dug into the shoulders of the road keep it out of bounds.

At Newton, a now station-less station village on the old Stratford and Huron Railway, turn south from County Road 6 onto Mornington Sideroad 9/10. At Mornington Concession 4/5 turn west to a pair of photogenic bridge abutments, one over the road and river, the other over the rusting rails of the Stratford and Huron Railway.

Continue west to Highway 19 and drive south into Milverton. At CPR Drive look for the vacant station grounds, and for New Form Manufacturing which was built when the railway arrived. The main street of Milverton, with its streetscaping and new businesses, exhibits the prosperity that it gained when the railway first arrived. Now follow Mill Street west from the main intersection in Milverton. When you come to a T intersection turn south and drive to County Road 6. Follow it west for twelve kilometres to Monkton.

While the heritage of Monkton's commercial core has fared poorly, it does contain an old-style feed mill beside the former station grounds on the west side of street. Opposite, the Elma Lodge occupies what was once a railway hotel. Best of all, however, you can still find the old station, a few blocks north and still in its original colours. It is now the office for a construction company.

As you drive west from Monkton you will be on Highway 23, but after two kilometres turn west onto Perth Road 9. From here almost to Blyth both highway and former railway run straight, mere yards apart. As you drive, picture an old steam train puffing along beside you. Head straight across country for 20 kilometres to Walton. On the way you will drive through some of Ontario's flattest and most fertile farmland. While following the old railway you are also on an old pioneer settlement road. And at Walton you will find one of those delightful old pioneer hotels. In operation since 1865, it is the Walton Inn Bed and Breakfast. On Walton's main street, just north of the hotel, sits a line of one time stores and shops, most now closed or in another use. The right of way and station grounds have been cleared and levelled, leaving behind little of Walton's railway heritage.

Perhaps the most railway-conscious town along the route is Blyth, home to the Blyth Theatrical Festival, where there is much railway heritage to see. On the CPR right of way, which crosses the main street north of the downtown area, you can see the Howson and Howson feed mill that dates from the days when everything was shipped by train. Opposite, on the north side of the roadbed, stands a structure that is even rarer than railway stations; the railway water tank. Despite being rusting and overgrown, it appears to be awaiting still the arrival of another steam engine.

Blyth boasts two surviving stations. The CPR station, the storey-and-a-half Plan 10 style that was repeated at Elmira and Wallenstein among others, now sits 1.5 kilometres south beside the Old Tannery Warehouse, a retail outlet for wool, leather, and fur products. The London Huron and Bruce (LHB) station lies one kilometre east of the main street along Dinsley Street. It is a small building which now offers bed and breakfast accommodation and displays a "witch's hat" roof atop the former waiting room.

While the right of way of the long abandoned LHB is no longer visible (it is not visible anywhere along its abandoned portion between Clinton and Wingham Junc-

Goderich's GG station was the largest "witch's hat" station built by the CPR, and the only one of brick. It still stands on site. (MTL)

tion), you can still walk to the high crossing over between it and the CPR by going east along the right of way from the water tank for about one kilometre. When the G&G arrived it simply burrowed through the earthen trestle that the LHB had earlier constructed. Although the tunnel has long since collapsed, a limestone culvert beside it still allows the creek to flow beneath the former LHB line. The CPR right of way is a snowmobile trail and so remains an transportation corridor with a decidedly historic flavour.

Drive west from Blyth on County Road 25, crossing the right of way on a bridge, for about ten kilometres to Auburn. The right of way itself twists and winds through high morainic hills passing creeks and woodlts and making for a pleasant hike.

At Auburn turn south at Sabo's Restaurant, which provides a welcome respite and home cooked meals, and drive through town. Both the highway and time have passed Auburn by. Old homes and stores line the former main street. The station, a two-storey building styled after the Dorking station with the hip gable on the second floor, stood one kilometre south on Mill Road, a location marked today by the Craig Hardwoods saw mill. A grain elevator stood across the track. The station was demolished in 1958.

From here, in dry weather, you can drive the roadbed for about two kilometres to the Maitland Road, an attractive drive along the wooded shore of the Maitland River that leads back into the village. Meanwhile, County Road 25 continues west through Carlow, a pioneer crossroads hamlet with a historic hotel, and on to Highway 21 which takes you south into Goderich.

This, the end of your route, is one of Ontario's most interesting towns. From its

octagonal main street to its octagonal jail (now a museum) you can see many preserved historic stores, institutions, and homes, as well as a pair of remarkable railway stations. The twin-towered former CNR still remains in use under the new and innovative ownership of the Goderich and Exeter Railway, a short line railway which operates the line into Stratford. It stands on East Street at Maitland.

When the giant CNR considered the branch line uneconomical, and proposed to abandon it, the short line company bought its line and proved that even small lines can make money.

The CPR station lies at the end of Harbour Street. As you follow West Street from the town square, you descend the lakeside cliff to the shore below. This marks the terminus of the old G&G. Although the many old warehouses and the water tank are gone, the station has been acquired by the town and survives. One of the most unusual in Ontario, the brick structure supports a witch's hat roof over what was the waiting room. After checking out the historic old building, continue along the shore road where you can enjoy a day on a newly landscaped beach park, or snack at a beachside snack bar.

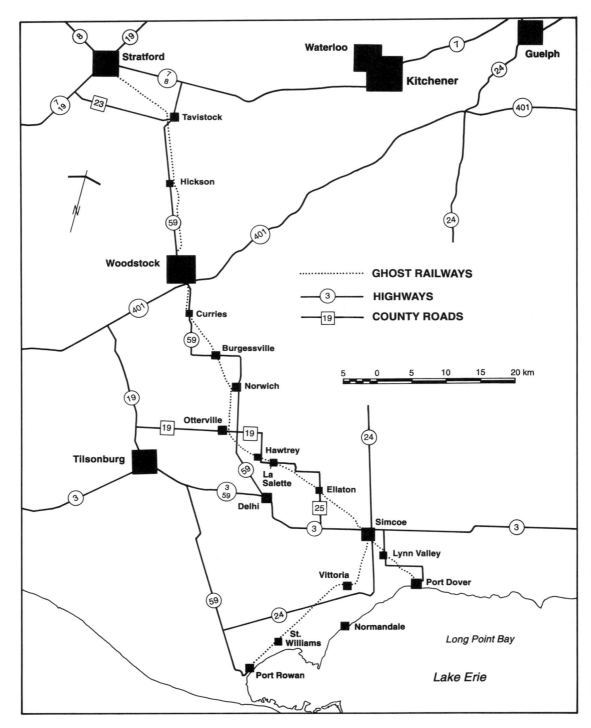

GHOST RAILWAYS

- .... GHOST RAILWAYS
- ③ —— HIGHWAYS
- 19 —— COUNTY ROADS

5 0 5 10 15 20 km

Stratford
Waterloo
Kitchener
Guelph
Tavistock
Hickson
Woodstock
Curries
Burgessville
Norwich
Otterville
Hawtrey
Tilsonburg
La Salette
Ellaton
Delhi
Simcoe
Lynn Valley
Port Dover
Vittoria
Normandale
St. Williams
Port Rowan
Long Point Bay
Lake Erie

CHAPTER ELEVEN

The Port Dover and Stratford: Of Fishing and Farming

Backgrounder

Except for a small segment, this is a line that has long been lost in Ontario's railway lore. When optimism reigned and plans had it going to Lake Huron, it was known as the Port Dover and Lake Huron. However, when it became evident that it would not pass beyond Stratford, it became the Port Dover and Stratford. Opened in 1876, its main line ran from Stratford via Tavistock to Simcoe and Port Dover with a short branch (known as the South Norfolk) to Port Rowan.

While it began as a separate line, its main role was as a feeder for major lines like the Wellington Grey and Bruce and the Grand Trunk. In 1881, the PDS, along with the Stratford and Huron that ran to Wiarton, and the Georgian Bay and Wellington (Palmerston to Durham), were amalgamated to form a railway with the lengthy name of Grand Trunk, Georgian Bay and Lake Erie Railway, in effect an affiliate of the Grand Trunk.

The land through which it passed is some of Canada's richest farmland. It is not surprising that the sidings and platforms of the PDS stations were piled with farm pro-

duce awaiting shipment, as passengers bustled from town to town to attend the many fairs and markets. A common sight beside many of the stations were cattle yards, grain elevators, and feed mills. In many of these communities today the feed mill is the only clue that a railway line even existed. CNR has sold most of the right of way to abutting property owners and only two short segments, between Hickson and Woodstock, and between Simcoe and Port Dover, have been retained as public trails.

Because it was the main railway town for the area, this route starts out in Stratford. While two earlier stations had stood in Stratford (the Grand Trunk/Buffalo and Lake Huron union station was at Guelph and Downie Streets, while the Port Dover and Lake Huron was on Falstaff at Nile), the current structure located at Shakespeare Street was built in 1913 and served the four lines that converged on the town. This handsome stone building still sees four Via passenger trains a day, as well as shipments along the fledgling Goderich and Exeter short line. Of the four lines that radiated from the festival town. The Port Dover and Stratford, and the once vital WGB line to Owen Sound were both abandoned, the latter in 1995.

All Aboard

To begin, drive east from the station to Romeo Street and turn south. At the corner of Norfolk Street you will see the end of a spur line, and in the distance the roof of the station you just left and the railway roundhouse. This now is as far as rail goes on the old PDS. The abandoned right of way continues on the east side of the road.

Between Stratford and Tavistock you will notice a recently abandoned right of way, not the original PDS, but the roadbed of the Buffalo Brantford and Goderich. The PDS was, in fact, abandoned in 1881 between the two communities after the BBG was built. Originally the line branched southward from Tavistock from a junction known as Tavistock Junction. All traces of this point have utterly vanished, as has most evidence of the line south to Hickson, which you can reach by following Highway 59 south from Tavistock.

Hickson's buildings are concentrated around the intersection of Highway 59 and County Road 8. The site of the railway crossing and the station, however is one kil-

A band livens up the opening ceremonies of the Otterville station museum.

ometre east. Look for the community library and the post office. The right of way is clear on the south side of the road but has been built over on the north side. Several of the stores that were built around the station, although no longer in business, survive and lend an historic air to the main street of this little town. The station was one of those attractive turreted depots. It was moved south of the village and, its turret having toppled, is now a house.

From the next road south of Hickson almost to Woodstock you can hike along the right of way. For ten kilometres it is the Hickson Nature Trail, a multi-purpose trail maintained by volunteers of the Woodstock Field Naturalists. Near the Kelsey Hayes foundry in west-end Woodstock, the roadbed is occupied by a now abandoned CPR spur.

The line wended its way through Woodstock by crossing Tecumseh Street north of Brant, and angling south east to Canterbury and Mary Streets. Subsequent housing developments have since obliterated the right of way. The line then passed down the centre of Huron Street, with a station at the southeast corner of Peel, and crossed the Grand Trunk line a block west of Burtch. In later years the through route was severed and a "Y" constructed at the CNR. New housing now covers this once vital junction as well. Take a moment, however, to visit the elegant Via station. Built by architect John Hobson of Great Western fame, this building has sheltered passengers since the 1880s, and is one of the oldest stations in Ontario in continuous passenger use. Fortunately, the structure has been designated for protection by Parks Canada.

Return to Highway 59 (Norwich Avenue) and drive south from Woodstock.

Clustered around the intersection of County Road 40 is the hamlet of Curries. One half kilometre south, notice the line of telephone poles and, on the east side of the road, a house with a lot at about a 45 degree angle to the road. These mark the right of way and the site of the Curries station. But other than the lonely line of poles and an occasional grassy mound, the right of way melds in with the fields and pastures only to re-emerge at Burgessville. Highway 59 carries you right into the small village where, east of Main Street, the Burgessville grain and feed mill marks the right of way and the site of the station. A 1920s CNR replacement of the original station, this small wooden depot outlasted the abandonment of the line, only to be later removed.

Highway 59 continues south to Norwich where the PDS intersected the Brantford Norfolk and Port Burwell Railway. The PDS crossed Main Street about 500 metres west of Highway 59 and was the site of the station. The busier line of the BNPB, later the CNR line, crossed Highway 59 just south of the main intersection and was the location of that more recent station. It was demolished in the 1970s. Norwich Junction, where the two lines crossed, is south of the village and eight kilometres west on County Road 5. With both lines now abandoned the only evidence that there was ever a railway operation here is a former hotel or boarding house on the south side of the road.

Of all the communities along the right of way, your next stop, Otterville, has best preserved and celebrated its railway heritage. Continue down Highway 59 to County Road 19 and drive west to Otterville. As you enter the village a municipal storage facility marks the original site of the railway and of the station. This simple and original board and batten structure stood here until 1991 when it was moved to become a museum a short distance west. After driving along the historic main street and past the old mill you will find the station, repainted in its Grand Trunk colours of grey and green, at the Erbtown historic site.

From Otterville the line swung sharply eastward to Hawtrey. This partial ghost town enjoyed two railway lines but didn't benefit much from either one. While the PDS angled across at the north end of the hamlet, where a store, school, sawmill, and a few houses clustered, the Canada Southern (later known as the Michigan Central), barged across at the south end. Here too a group of buildings clustered around the station grounds.

The Hawtrey station outlasted the demise of the railway until the early 1980s when, derelict, it was demolished. Nearby, the old store and school still stand although neither enjoys its original use. A short side street marks the approximate location of the now vanished right of way.

A short distance east at La Salette, the line crossed the still active Michigan Central. A crossing tower and a station both stood at the location, although today there is no evidence to mark the spot. The village remains a lively, rural residential community. The line then heads out once more to cross the flat farm fields, forging the misnamed Big Creek on a small trestle, to Simcoe.

A prosperous farm town, Simcoe was also the focus of three railway lines, the Canada Air Line (now CNR), the Lake

The branch line to Port Rowan passed this large station at St. Williams. (OA)

Erie and Northern, and the PDS. The PDS crossed the Air Line at a point two kilometres west of the CNR station (today a yellow Atco station). It then followed Metcalfe south through the town. Near Victoria Street the line split, the main portion, marked by a line of elevators, veering easterly toward Port Dover, a branch line veering southwest to Port Rowan.

To follow the branch line continue south through Simcoe on Highway 24 to Vittoria Road and drive west. The pre-confederation capital of London District, Vittoria is now a ghost town that has returned to life. While old sidewalks lead past the few commercial buildings left from its heady administrative days, all around the town new houses are appearing. The right of way is most visible beside the road to the community centre north of the main street.

Follow County Road 58 south to Highway 24 and drive west to Walsh Station, where the railway's only legacy lies in the name. Continue west on Highway 24 to County Road 16 which leads you south to St. Williams. Although the place retains a few historic structures, the right of way is now all but lost, the only evidence being beside the community church. In Port Rowan, seven kilometres west of St. Williams on Regional Road 42 and the terminus of this branch, you may see the feed mill and the onetime freight shed of the railway on the east side of the road.

To return to the main line east of Simcoe you can leave your car and follow the right of way on foot or bicycle. The Lyn Valley Trail is maintained by the Region of Haldimand-Norfolk and follows the twisting right of way along the shady banks of the Lyn River into the town of Port Dover. The Historic Atlas of Norfolk County describes the town as being "the terminus of the Port Dover and Lake Huron (as the PDS was originally called) and as such ... likely to become a place of great importance." And so it did, with railway facilities, and industries and fishing operations around the harbour.

The line ends today near the former Port Dover railway station. A post-World War II building with a flat roof, it stands at the end of McNab near Patrick Street and is used, unflatteringly, as a storage facility. The original line continued to the lake, following Bridge and Harbour Streets. The older station is slightly better cared for. It stands on Walker Street not far from its original site, and although it has lost one of its ends, it has been repainted in railway red. Port Dover is a place where you can walk the sands of Lake Erie's beaches and watch the squat white fishing boats that still rumble to and from the new government wharf. However, the railway days of the town and the railway that took its name have vanished forever.

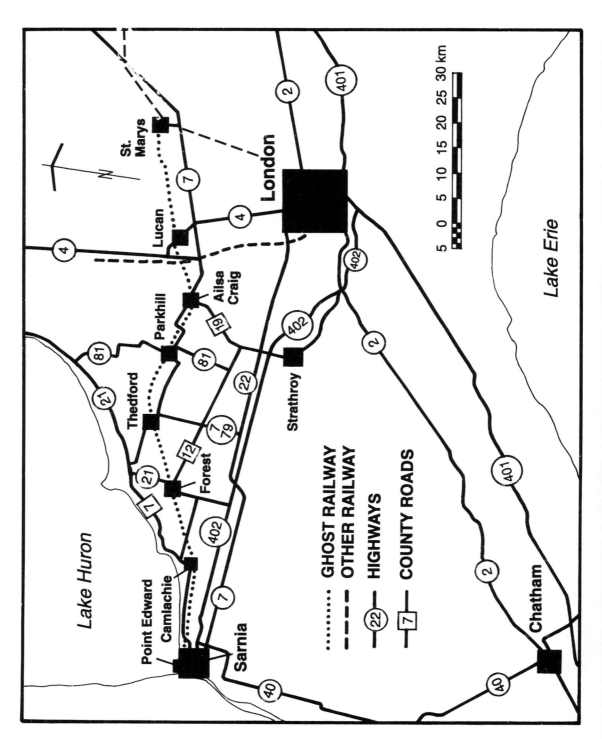

Lake Huron

Lake Erie

St. Marys

London

Lucan

Ailsa Craig

Parkhill

Thedford

Forest

Strathroy

Point Edward
Camlachie

Sarnia

Chatham

5 0 5 10 15 20 25 30 km

N

GHOST RAILWAY
OTHER RAILWAY
HIGHWAYS
COUNTY ROADS

⋯⋯⋯
– – –
22
7

CHAPTER TWELVE

The Grand Trunk West: St. Mary's to Sarnia

Backgrounder

Next to the CPR the most important railway in the formation of Canada was the Grand Trunk. Just as the CPR linked the nation from sea to sea in the 1880s, the Grand Trunk linked pre-confederation Canada in the 1850s.

By 1860 this British financed venture could claim a network that stretched from Levis, opposite Quebec City, from which point the Intercolonial Railway ran to Halifax, to Point Edward, a mile north of Sarnia, and an all-important connection to Chicago. The Grand Trunk's main rival, the Great Western, admittedly had crossed southwestern Ontario first, running from Niagara Falls to Sarnia and Windsor, but it was primarily an Ontario short-cut for American railway interests.

East of Toronto the GT line followed the shore of Lake Ontario to Kingston and the St. Lawrence to Montreal. West of Toronto it ran west to Kitchener and Stratford and then to Point Edward through the communities of Lucan, Parkhill, Thedford, and Forest. In 1882 the GT absorbed the Great Western network, giving it a spider's web of railway lines enmeshing all of south-ern Ontario and focussing on one main line to Windsor and two to Sarnia.

In the pre-automotive era this density was not a problem. The railway was the province's economic lifeline, and towns that developed along its lines were guaranteed prosperity. Following World War II, the rampant surge of highway development and truck traffic and the modernization of the railway technology reduced the shining rails to rusting steel, silent and useless. Many of these lines became uneconomical and were downgraded and eventually abandoned altogether.

The original GT route between Toronto and Montreal (albeit realigned in a few places) remains one of Canada's busiest pieces of railway trackage, carrying several freight and passenger trains every day. West of Toronto, while the former Great Western route carries the most CNR and Via trains, the old GT line to Kitchener and Stratford also remains busy. West of St. Mary's, however, it is a different story. From St. Mary's Junction, just a mile north of the town on its Point Edward main line, the GT had run a line south to join the Great Western at London. Today all trains follow that southerly route while the historic old GT main line from St. Mary's to Point Edward now lies abandoned.

In 1982 the first section, from Sarnia to Forest, was abandoned leaving the once vital line a mere stub. By 1989 it was cut back to Lucan and today is only a memory. The short time that has lapsed since abandonment has not yet erased all traces of the line's heritage, however, and much can yet be seen by following the old route by car.

All Aboard

It is fitting that one of Ontario's most historic towns, St. Mary's, can claim the old line's most historic building. This town of stone, widely known for its spectacular town hall, opera house, and main street bridge, also boasts the oldest railway station in western Ontario, it too made of stone, of course.

Junction Station was constructed in 1857 in the distinctive GT style that made its stations among Canada's most attractive and durable. A pattern popular in England in the 1840s, the limestone building incorporates seven stone arch windows along both front and back, and two on each end. The low wide roof is punctuated by four chim-

The stone station at St Mary's junction sits neglected, although it is western Ontario's oldest standing station.

neys. Common between Toronto and Montreal, the style was little used west of Toronto, although two examples do survive outside Ontario, on the Grand Trunk Western in Michigan. Built in Port Huron and Mount Clemens, both are elegantly preserved and serve as an example to Ontario municipalities.

All three stations — Port Huron, Mount Clemens and St. Mary's Junction — played a role in the life of noted American inventor, Thomas Edison. While he sold newspapers from the Port Huron station, and rescued from an onrushing freight train the infant son of the station agent in Mount Clemens, his experience at St. Mary's Junction was less praiseworthy. For it was here

that as night operator, he devised an electronic means of fooling his dispatcher into believing he was on duty, while he was in fact sleeping. Had his ruse remained undetected, he may never have hurried back to the U.S., under threat of criminal prosecution, to become one of the world's most prolific inventors.

Unlike the restored Grand Trunk depots in Port Huron and Mount Clemens, the one in St. Mary's remains in poor repair. Although its historic status has been recognized through a plaque erected by Parks Canada, it remains neglected and vandalized, surrounded by a chain-link fence and an overgrown field. Part of the blame lies in the indifference of local authorities and

By contrast, the Grand Trunk station in Port Huron Michigan has been preserved,
a lesson to their Canadian neighbours.

part in the antipathy of CNR, the landowner, which has routinely displayed disdain towards its own contribution to the heritage of Canada.

To reach the station, follow Church Street north from the town hall in downtown St. Mary's to the river and turn right past the bridge. Drive a further 1.5 kilometres to a sign that indicates "Junction Station," and follow that road for another 500 metres. The line that passes in front of the station remains in use and is busy, so take care when near it. Just a few metres south, however, the historic main line to Point Edward sits overgrown and barely discernible. Gone too is the old railway workers' settlement that once made the junction a busy community.

Highway 7 leads west from St. Mary's to County Road 23. Four kilometres north is Granton. A creation of the GT, Granton consists of a grid network of streets that were laid out on the north side of the tracks by the Grant brothers — William, Alexander, and James. Following the arrival of the railway, a debate erupted over the naming of the town. The Grants favoured "Granton" while others wanted "Amwik," a native word meaning "beaver." While the present name won the day the residents on the south side of the track continued to use Amwik.

Granton was able to boast three stores, two hotels, a pair of churches, and a saw and grist mill. Because the railway has been so recently removed, much of its landscape is still evident. The roadbed remains clearly visible, the station grounds on the north side now a vacant field, while a feed mill still stands on the south side. The churches, homes, and a few of the commercial operations survive on the village streets. The old wooden station itself sits deteriorating in a field on the west side of County Road 23 one half kilometre south of the village.

Highway 7 then leads on to Lucan. According to one 19th century writer, Lucan was a "place of very little importance until the GT was opened since which time its growth has been extremely rapid." Lucan quickly acquired several mills, stores, and hotels, as well as an unsavoury reputation. The same writer acerbically noted that "the welfare of the place has of late been imperilled by the unfortunate exhibitions of malice which have lately culminated in incendiary fires which have checked for a time the progress of the village."

More commonly known as the "Black Donnelly Feud," this bitter rivalry pitted families of Irish immigrants against each other. Beatings and burnings were often attributed to one large clan, the Donnellys. These "exhibitions of malice" exploded on a cold night in February, 1880, when a group of vigilantes burst into the Donnelly home and brutally murdered five members of the clan. While several local residents, including the constable, stood trial, none was convicted. The Donnelly grave, which sombrely lists the victims simply as having "died" (the original gravestone bluntly said "murdered"), sits in the yard of St. Patrick's Church a few kilometres east of the town.

While most of Lucan's commercial establishments are along what is today Highway 7, the station and the railside industries were several blocks west where feed mills still recall the railway landscape. The old depot, like the others along the GT line, has long been removed.

To stay close to the right of way follow County Road 13 west from the main intersection in the village to County Road 22 and turn south. A short distance south, and clearly visible on the west side of the road, are the abutments of the small GT bridge that crossed over the former London Huron and Bruce Railway, a line that originated in London and ran north to Wingham. CNR later acquired the line and cut back the tracks to between Exeter and Goderich, a segment which remains in use by the Goderich and Exeter short line.

County Road 22 continues south to Highway 7, which leads west to Ailsa Craig, the next village to owe its origin to the GT. Laid out on lands subdivided by David Craig, the village added the Atkinson and Smith mills, and was for a number of years the leading cattle market west of London. The GT roadbed angles across Highway 7 at the west end of the small downtown area. On the north side of the street are the feed mills once served by GT sidings. A short distance north of the main intersection stands a simple former railway hotel, now a residence.

Highway 7 continues to follow the GT westward to the historic community of Parkhill. Prior to 1865, Parkhill, known variously as "Westwood" and "Swainby," had only five houses. The opportunities offered by the GT combined with excellent water power on Mud Creek to induce Harrison and Harris to erect larger grist and flour mills. Other industries followed and soon Parkhill could claim a large bustling downtown of sturdy brick stores, as well as a newspaper, the *Parkhill Gazette*.

The GT cut straight through the middle of that downtown, its station grounds and industrial sites now vacant. A row of 19th century buildings line King Street beside the right of way, among them the offices of the Gazette. Although the community is re-storing its historic vitality by renovating the downtown with such features as vintage streetlights, the only real trace of its once thriving railway is in the name of the street that leads to the station, Station Street.

But of all the villages and towns spawned by the GT it is perhaps in Thedford that the townscape itself was most dictated by the railway. To reach it follow Highway 7 west from Parkhill to Highway 79 north which becomes Thedford's main street, the site of the town's railway heritage. While the south side of the road is lined with commercial buildings, the north side stretches away as a vacant field. Where dirt and cinders now lie bare, were once the station, the tracks, and the industries of the days of rail.

The GT originally named the place Widder Station, after a nearby settlement. But, at the insistence of the farmer who had donated land for the station grounds, the name was subsequently changed. The old name lingers on to the east of town, however. A local road bears the name, as does a golf course where a club house was built in the style of a Grand Trunk railway station.

The railway attracted the flour and grist mills of the Kennedy brothers, as well as John Cameron's woollen works, Edward Johnson's carriage works, and a pair of hotels. Thus Thedford's population quickly reached 600. Although the station and the tracks are all gone now an unusual vestige lingers: an ancient stone warehouse with the words "Grand Trunk Storage" on the side. If all other vestiges of the railway heritage have vanished, this sole survivor should at least be saved from oblivion.

Forest, the next GT community, also contains a replica station. Follow Highway 79 west of Thedford to County Road 6, west to Highway 21, and then south to Forest.

Prior to the arrival of the railway, there was little here except John Woodruff's general store. Then, as a contemporary writer noted, the town was "ushered into existence by the construction of the railway." Named for the lush woodlands which at that time surrounded it, Forest's population grew to 1800 and, thanks to the railway, became the grain shipping centre of southwestern Ontario. In 1888, when the town was only a few residents short of the 2000 required to legally become a "town," Grand Trunk officials agreed to allow a train full of passengers to sit at the station until they too could be counted and give the place the magic number it needed to gain that status.

Following abandonment of the line west of this point, Forest remained for a number of years the end of the line from St. Mary's. Stores and offices have been placed on the old right of way in the downtown. To the northeast, however, the roadbed has become a trail that runs across farm fields all the way to Ailsa Craig.

While the place continues to be a prosperous commercial centre for the surrounding region, now denuded of its forest, its railway roots have not been entirely forgotten. Travel a few blocks west of Highway 21 to the town library. Here, near the site of the original Forest station, the library

The Forest library recaptures the flavour of the town's old station.

was built to an almost exact plan of that station. With its trade mark Grand Trunk tower, it invokes the railway heritage of a community that owes its existence to the Grand Trunk.

From Forest to Camlachie the roadbed traverses flat farmlands; much of it is ploughed under, and traceable only by fence rows and tree lines. At Camlachie, a small GT hamlet, a feed mill marks the one-time train line. But from Camlachie almost as far as Sarnia the abandoned railway line has been converted into a public trail. Created in 1988, the 16-kilometre Howard Watson Nature Trail is managed by the Lambton County Wildlife Inc., a member club of the Federation of Ontario Naturalists.

But it was not created without a fight. Although the abandoned roadbed had been used by nature walkers for some time, the township council of the day preferred to sell it to adjacent owners. When that did not show promise of profit to the township, council agreed to let the wildlife group assume responsibility for maintaining the trail. Today the trail, which passes through extensive natural areas, is popular with students of biology as well as with hikers, bikers, and cross-country skiers.

Point Edward "owes its inception and growth to being the western Canadian terminus of the GT," noted the Atlas of Lambton County in 1880. It was "selected because the current [in the St Clair River] is so swift as to prevent freezing... The passenger depot is a handsome and capacious white brick structure possessing the most ap-

proved modern conveniences including dining and refreshment rooms." Beside the depot were two grain elevators, freight sheds, train yards, stock yards, repair shops, and a 21-stall roundhouse. The town "is exclusively a railway town composed absolutely of GT employees and families," continued the author of the atlas. Of the more than 1400 residents, fully 425 were railway employees. A street railway connected the point to Sarnia, more than a mile away.

After it absorbed the Great Western in 1882, the Grand Trunk began construction of the St. Clair River tunnel in Sarnia. Once completed, this engineering marvel made Point Edward all but redundant. With the end of the barge era, the Grand Trunk's once busy terminus became little more than a transshipment point.

Today the tracks have been lifted, the right of way built over, and the yards, the shops, roundhouse, and depot long demolished. The station grounds have become an overgrown field, likely soon to be redeveloped. Below the looming Blue Water Bridge to the U.S., the only evidence that Point Edward was ever a railway town is the former CNR freight shed, abandoned and slated for removal.

While Point Edward's railway heritage, indeed much of that along Canada's first "national" railway, disappears into the mists of time, Port Huron on the opposite shore has managed to preserve its tiny and original Grand Trunk station. Beside it is a plaque to commemorate inventor Thomas Edison, who as a youth sold newspapers from this depot.

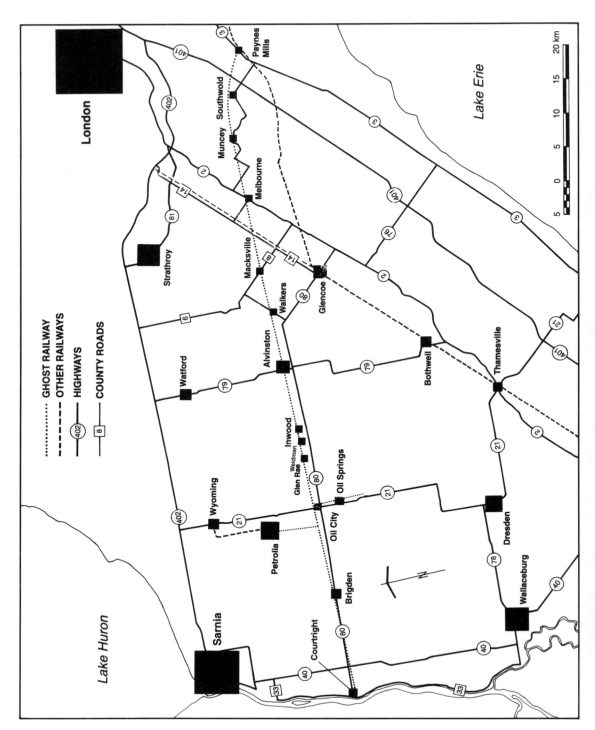

CHAPTER THIRTEEN

The Canada Southern: Land of the Black Gold

Backgrounder

A lonely line of hydro poles marches across the flat green farmlands to a nearly treeless horizon. Until 1960 the onlooker would have seen plumes of smoke belching from the stacks of steam engines, or exhaust from diesels, followed by the long, low silhouettes of boxcars or passenger coaches.

This was the line of the Canada Southern Railway (CSR), St. Clair Branch.

It was just one of several Ontario railway lines whose founders saw as a convenient short-cut between American cities, in this case Chicago and Buffalo. Yet it was launched by Canadians William Thompson and Adam Crooke, although most of their efforts were spent in the U.S. looking for interest, and money, from American financiers.

While the main line of the CSR ran almost arrow straight from Niagara Falls to Windsor, the St. Clair Branch veered northwestward from a junction just west of St. Thomas and continued to the St. Clair River. Here, at a point the railway called Courtright, after Milton Courtright, the railway's principal financial contributor, the

railway had hoped to establish a major railway terminus, with a bridge to carry traffic across the busy river to St. Clair on the Michigan side. From there the trains would make their way to Chicago, the gateway to the American West.

The American link failed, however, and the Windsor route with its tunnel under the Detroit River earned the bulk of the traffic. The grand scheme of a bridge over the St. Clair was reduced to a mere barge. It operated across the river between Courtright and St. Clair for a few years until it burned and sank. With it sank the last vestige of the failed American link.

The CSR pinned its early hopes for revenue on the oil boom that in the 1860s put places like Oil Springs and Petrolia on the map. To provide easier access to these prospering places, a new line, the Chatham Sarnia and Erie (CSE), was created. Originating at a place called Shrewsbury on Lake Erie, it was intended to pass through Oil Springs and Petrolia and terminate at Sarnia; however, the project never went beyond short spurs from the St. Clair Branch south to Oil Springs and north to Petrolia.

Later, when the oil industry moved to Sarnia, the CSE was absorbed by the Canada Southern, which rerouted the unbuilt section to bypass the oil fields and follow instead the St. Clair River into Sarnia. Finally, in 1960, the whistles fell silent on the St. Clair Branch, and the smoke evaporated forever from the horizon. The track was lifted and the stations removed.

All Aboard

While the CSR may have gained little revenue from this branch it left a lasting imprint on the landscape. Because the terrain through which the route passed is level and of deep soil, no rock cuts and few causeways were needed. Several impressive bridges, however, were put across the rivers and gullies that traverse this part of the province. Much of the old roadbed has reverted to farmland, defined in places only by the hydro towers that follow it.

Instead, the main legacy of the CSR's St. Clair branch lies in the weathered old railway towns and villages that boomed along

The Oil Springs station now rests on the grounds of the museum and the site of North America's first commercial oil well.

the route, feeding off the shipping of grain and lumber.

The main line through St. Thomas now carries the freight trains of its new corporate owner, CNR. Ten kilometres west of St. Thomas, nearly indistinguishable from the sprawl along Highway 3, lies the one-time mill town of Paynes Mill. Here the St. Clair branch left the main line to make its way westward. The roadbed, however, is a mere mound that is visible only where it crosses the highway a few metres east of County Road 45.

Southwold Station, however, is more distinctive. This hamlet that grew around the station sits on County Road 19 at County Road 17, where the pavement ends two kilometres north of Highway 401. The small, weathered buildings have seen better days. One is the old railway hotel that until recently housed a small general store. Just to the east a row of hydro towers looms across the road, marking the railway roadbed and the site of the long-vanished station.

The hamlet of Muncy, originally Delaware Station, on County Road 11, marks the location of the line's second largest bridge, that over the Thames River. Here, on the north side of the road, look for the high embankments that carried the trains of the CSR over Southwestern Ontario's longest river. The trestle has gone leaving only the abutments and the embankments.

The second largest settlement along the line is Melbourne. Originally a busy farm crossroads hamlet named Ekfrid, it boomed with the coming of the railway and was surveyed into streets and town lots. After enduring a series of different names, Longwood and Wendigo among them, the place was finally named Melbourne in 1887. At the intersection of Highway 2 and County Road 9, it remains to this day a busy focus for the local farm community. But railway days were busier days, a time when trains passed through the east end of the community, paused at the station or feed mill, and then puffed off.

The right of way is clearly marked as a cinder driveway, with the hydro towers beside it. The Caramet mill has survived the passing of train service and stands on Elizabeth Street which was laid out parallel to the tracks. As the St. Clair branch headed westward it intersected the tracks of both the CNR (originally the Great Western,

The Grand Trunk's Petrolia station still stands, now a library, its grand style commemorating the town's former status as the oil capital of the world.

and then the Grand Trunk) and the CPR. These crossings, invisible today, occurred within a couple of miles of each other west of Melbourne.

Save for an abandoned general store, the tiny station hamlet of Mackville would be invisible as well. The original Mackville consists of a few structures around a crossroads seven kilometres north of Highway 2 on County Road 8. The old store, one half kilometre past that, marks the CSR crossing. The still present hydro towers are the only giveaway.

Another abandoned general store and a handful of houses announce Walkers, the next station stop for the CSR, one kilome-tre south of County Road 2 and about four kilometres west of County Road 8. Surrounded by farms, the old wooden store with its porch now silent displays a tranquillity that belies the busier railway era, when several trains a day would bellow their throaty whistle and puff to a halt at the small wooden station a few yards east of the store.

A kilometre and a half further west lies Highway 80, the route that leads to Alvinston, the most architecturally interesting village on the branch. Before the railway came, Alvinston barely existed. It began as a mill settlement known as Brooke Mills. As the atlas of 1880 describes it, "the settle-

The beautiful Courtright Tavern was built during the railway's grander days.

ment was very slow until after the building of the CSR. Its completion in 1871 gave a decided impulse to development." Mills and foundries flocked to railside and the settlement boomed to a population of 900. The railway erected its largest bridge here across the Sydenham River.

But Alvinston gained from not just one, but two railway lines. Shortly after the CSR opened up its St. Clair branch, the Grand Trunk decided to link its new main line to Sarnia (which it had acquired from the Great Western) and that to Windsor (another Great Western acquisition). Stores and hotels appeared along its main street as the town became the focus of the eastern part of the county. Many heritage stores still stand on the main street, the most interesting being the Grand Central Hotel across the street from the Columbia Tavern, both landmarks from the prosperous railway era. While the railways are long gone, the intersection of the two lines can be clearly seen from River Street south of South Railway Street. Here the CSR roadbed follows a trench while the abutments of the Grand Trunk bridge guard the two sides.

The site of the former CSR station is now just a vacant lot a short distance to the west of the crossing. The Grand Trunk station stood on Lorne Street, a location now dominated by a feed mill. The old CSR station was removed to farm field where it blew down in a wind storm, while the GT station survived the end of that railway only to be removed to make way for an enlargement of the mill.

The next station stop to the west is pure railway. Inwood's stores, its street pattern, its one former hotel, indeed its very existence, are all due to the CSR. But its origins are suspicious, to say the least. While

Milton Courtwright was laying out his railway in the 1870s, his nephew James, along with two partners, purchased 95 acres of land on the proposed route and subdivided the tract into town lots, naming it after a village on the Hudson River in New York state. Howls of protest and shrieks of "conflict of interest" would reverberate over such an arrangement today.

The place was the site of a large stave and saw mill until the forest cover was depleted; it then took its place as an important shipper of farm produce. Situated a kilometre and a half north of Highway 80 on County Road 8, Inwood's main street parallels the old roadbed, which is still indicated by the hydro towers. The feed mill built beside the site of the station dominates the landscape while across the road, on the west side of County Road 8, is the two-storey red-brick building that was once the railway hotel. Inwood's railway legacy lingers in the names of three of its streets: Courtright, Holmes, and Moore, Inwood's founders.

A short distance west, the two former farm sidings of Weidman and Glen Rae have vanished completely, leaving only their names on a few maps.

Oil Springs, on the other hand, appeared on more than a few world maps in the middle of the last century. At this now quiet location the discovery of a gooey black substance in the ground in 1852 brought about the world's first oil boom. But when the oil men moved north to Petrolia as ever richer discoveries were made, Oil Springs declined and in the words of the 1880 atlas, became almost a "deserted village." The atlas continues: "Among the many instances of rapid growth and subsequent decay, no place in Canada stands out so prominently as Oil Springs." Its population plunged from more than 4000 to less than 300 in just ten years: "The town has a most dilapidated and forlorn appearance; houses in all stages of ruin and decay...." But in the 1870s the CSR construction crews drew ever closer, "inspiring the capitalists with fresh vigour."

However, the line passed to the north, through Oil City. A purely speculative venture, the site of Oil City had been acquired by American land venturers in 1852. But when the oil boom moved north to Petrolia, the speculators went bankrupt and the townsite reverted to the government. In 1864 another group of speculators tried,

but within two years they too had failed. Its third life was more successful when, after the CSR established a station, it managed to attract a pair of stores, a hotel, a few industries, and one hundred inhabitants. But Oil Springs was not forgotten altogether. A spur was built to it along the route of the proposed CSE.

Despite the 35-year absence of trains, the area's railway heritage is still firmly embedded in the landscape. Oil City sits at the intersection of Highways 80 and 21. A short distance north, Thistle Street branches east and follows the railway roadbed to its intersection with Main Street. While the town plan created by the speculators is evident in

The Courtwright station marked the terminus of the CSR.

the grid network of streets, most of the building lots remained vacant until the country living boom of the last two or three decades filled them with newer housing.

South on Highway 21 lies Oil Springs, once the world's most important oil town. Despite the eventual arrival of the railway, the streets remain quiet, the only vestige of those headier times being the lettering on the former oil supply store one block south. It is this road that leads also to the location of the world's first commercial well, the Oil Springs museum.

A modern structure, the museum contains artifacts and offers videos that interpret this all-but-forgotten chapter in Ontario's history. And it hasn't forgotten the railway: on the museum grounds the former Oil Springs station, resplendent in its fresh coat of green paint, contains railway paraphernalia and photographs from the CSR, and is the best celebration of the railway's heritage anywhere along the line.

Meanwhile, ten kilometres to the north of Oil City, on another CSR spur, Petrolia enjoyed the oil boom and the prosperity that was denied its neighbour further south. This is evident in Petrolia's many mansions and grand town hall. Originally spelt "Petrolea," the present incorrect spelling has been attributed by some authors to an early "clerical error."

The CSR spur has been absorbed by Petrolia's road system. While the former CSR station, a wooden structure with a single turret, was moved to Bright's Grove on Lake Huron to became a summer home, that built by the Grand Trunk on its spur

line from the north has been revitalized as the town library, its brick towers a main street landmark.

Brigden, the next town west of Oil City, grew as "an important station on the CSR," according to the 1880 atlas. With the arrival of the CSR, stores and hotels, mills and foundries appeared on the town plot that Nathaniel Boswell had laid out. He named it after John Brigden, an early railway engineer. The right of way is still clear as it makes its way through town a few yards north of the highway, and on First Street it still passes the feed mill that dates back to train times.

Highway 80 ends in Courtright, the original terminus of the CSR. While what is today the Chessie System (CSX) railway line still passes from south to north through the town a few blocks east of the river, the CSR terminus was located on the waterfront. The 1880 atlas confirms this location: the "terminal facilities of the CSR are extensive and complete, a large steam ferry plies continuously."

Little remains from that heady era. The entire waterfront is now part of a pleasant park and marina provided by the St. Clair Parks Commission. Despite its pleasant ambience, the park contains nothing to remind visitors of the railway that created the village in the first place. But you can find evidence of the railway in a couple of places. In the south end of town a pattern of curving streets follows the alignment of the railway right of way. And opposite the park stands the aging railway hotel that is now the Courtright Tavern, displaying a grandeur that today seems out of place.

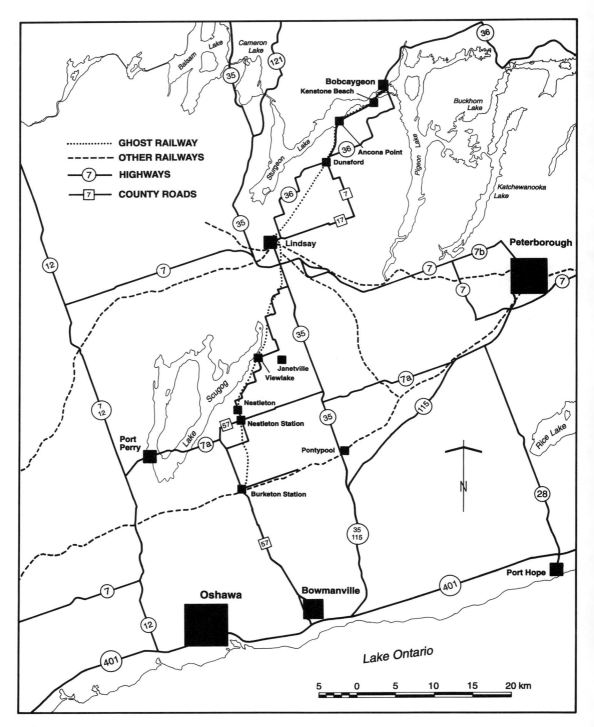

Legend

- GHOST RAILWAY
- OTHER RAILWAYS
- HIGHWAYS
- COUNTY ROADS

Balsam Lake
Cameron Lake
121
35
Bobcaygeon
Kenstone Beach
Buckhorn Lake
36
Sturgeon Lake
Ancona Point
Dunsford
36
7
17
Pigeon Lake
Katchewanooka Lake
35
Lindsay
Peterborough
12
7
7b
7
7
7
35
Janetville
Viewlake
7a
Scugog Lake
Nestleton
115
Rice Lake
57
Nestleton Station
35
Port Perry
7 12
7a
Pontypool
28
N
Burketon Station
35 115
57
Port Hope
Oshawa
Bowmanville
401
12
7
401
Lake Ontario

5 0 5 10 15 20 km

CHAPTER FOURTEEN

The Lindsay Bobcaygeon and Pontypool: Into the Kawarthas

Backgrounder

Another pair of the spokes in Lindsay's hub belonged to a short and short-lived line known at first as the Bobcaygeon, Lindsay and Pontypool railway.

Soon after its inception in 1890 by a group of Lindsay businessmen, the line lost its name and became part of the CPR's rapidly expanding network of southern Ontario railway lines. Despite its name, the line did not originate at Pontypool (a small community southeast of Lindsay) but rather at Burketon, several kilometres to the west.

The route followed the southern shores of the Scugog Lake and River into Lindsay, and then led northeastward to Bobcaygeon, a busy and historic tourist town on the shore of the Trent Canal. While the southern portion of the line between Lindsay and Burketon was abandoned in 1933 after just forty years of operation, the route to Bobcaygeon managed to linger on until 1961.

Because of its late arrival and relatively light traffic, the line had little impact upon the landscape through which it passed. Nevertheless, there remain a few intriguing villages, road alignments, and buildings for the explorer to find.

All Aboard

The hamlet of Burketon Station nestles in the sand hills of the Great Oak Ridges Moraine, less than one kilometre west of Durham Road 57, about 12 kilometres north of Bowmanville. This junction point between the CPR's Ontario and Quebec line and the Lindsay and Bobcaygeon branch lay little known to outsiders until the 1970s, when the beauty of the hills that surround it began to attract a new generation of country dwellers.

The core of the hamlet, however, still contains many of its railway houses, although many have shed their traditional insulbrick siding in favour of aluminum and vinyl. The two-storey station which stood east of the main street on the north side of the track is long gone, although the "Y" which marked the location of the connection to Lindsay is still evident. North of Burketon, the right of way has reverted to farm fields and is all but invisible.

Nestleton Station, on Highway 7A about 10 kilometres north of Burketon, was the station site chosen for the hamlet of Nestleton about one kilometre to the north. The railside village soon outgrew its parent and today still contains the shady side streets lined with the large houses that were built when the railway arrived. The right of way crossed the highway at the site of the convenience store at the corner of Nestleton Road. The station itself, located just south of the store, outlasted the demise of the

line by half a century, surviving as a house until the mid 1980s when the owners decided to build a new home and removed the old station.

Two kilometres north of Nestleton Station, Nestleton Road intersects Durham Regional Road 57. Here the nearly invisible right of way parallels the road for a short distance about one kilometre east of the intersection. Turn right and follow Regional Road 57.

About seven kilometres northeast of the junction lies the hamlet of Viewlake. Now a collection of country homes and cottages, this was the location for the railway's Janetville station. A simple frame building,

Gone and largely forgotten are the days when trains still stopped at Bobcaygeon's station. (DS)

it stood empty on its original site also for half a century following the removal of the line, and was used for a time as a trappers' cabin. It burned down in the late 1980s. The station stood where Regional Road 57 swings east; Janetville, the pioneer village after which the station took its name, lies about four kilometres to the east.

Follow road 57 east for one kilometre then turn north along a sideroad leading to a T intersection where you jog west slightly before returning north. This route zig zags for about seven kilometres, roughly paralleling the Scugog River to Highway 35. Look for some bridge and causeway remnants over a creek at the 5.5 kilometre mark.

From here into Lindsay the line vanishes once again. South of Lindsay it joined another CPR branch line, known as the Georgian Bay and Seaboard Railway at a place called Lindsay Junction (the site can be found on Logie Street), and followed that trackage to the site of the old CPR station near Colborne Street in the north end of the town. The section from Lindsay to Bobcaygeon lasted until 1961, and parts remain quite visible. In Lindsay itself a spur line served some local industries in the northeast section of the town until around 1990.

From Lindsay to Dunsford, field and swamps have largely reclaimed the old line. However, it re-emerges as a dry weather trail for about three kilometres west of Dunsford. The village of Dunsford, located at Highway 36 and Victoria Road 7, owes much of its growth to the railway. The right of way is still clear through the village and a feed mill, once served by the line, still stands. The Dunsford station, the only station to survive on this line, was moved about two kilometres east to Emily Creek where it now serves, much in its original condition, as a summer home.

East of Dunsford, Victoria Road 24 follows the right of way for a scenic eight kilometres into the historic lakeland town of Bobcaygeon and shows why this portion of the route was popular with tourists. As it nears Bobcaygeon, picturesque Sturgeon Lake comes into view. The road passes summer retreats like Birch Point and Kenstone Beach, where cottagers or tourists would tumble off the train at the shed-sized flag stop stations to enjoy the breezes and the waters of the Kawarthas.

The road then swings into Bobcaygeon where, at the corner of Mansfield and Park Streets the one-and-a-half storey wooden station once stood. Aside from the road itself, the only vestige of railway days in Bobcaygeon is the feed mill which still stands at this location. Bobcaygeon began as a mill town in the 1830s and boomed with the addition of the Trent Canal. Historic sites like the lock station on the Trent Canal, the Boyd mansion, and the limestone bank at the main intersection, all pre-date the days of the railway; today, however, you must come by car.

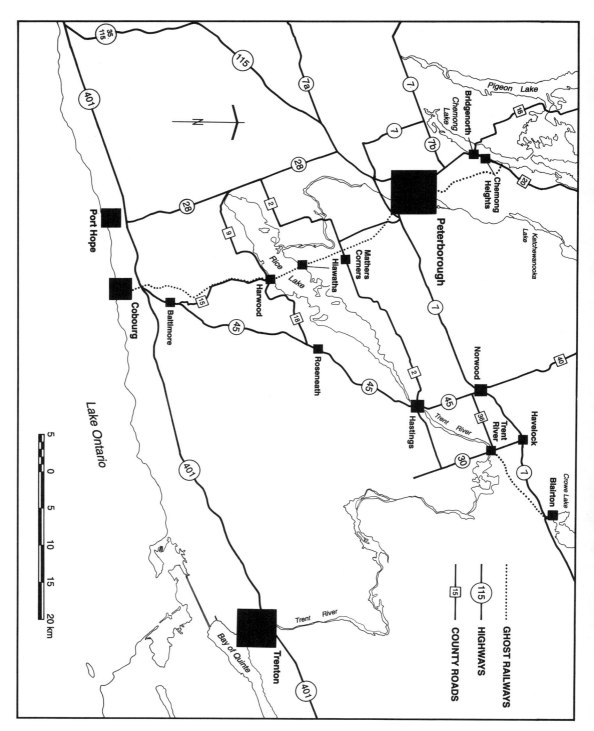

CHAPTER FIFTEEN

Rails Over Rice Lake:
The Cobourg and Peterborough Railway

Backgrounder

Incorporated in 1834 as the Cobourg Railroad Company, the Cobourg and Peterborough Railway (C&P) was one of Ontario's first chartered railways; it was also one of the first to be abandoned. But it is the relics of this ill-fated attempt to cross Rice Lake that have survived and remain one of Ontario's railway oddities.

Most of Ontario's first railways fed into steamer travel rather than replacing it. From the tiny ports on Lakes Ontario and Erie, railway lines snaked inland to bring out lumber and farm produce. Two such ports, only eight miles apart and fiercely competetive, were Port Hope and Cobourg, each anxious to be first to tap that hinterland. Nearly twenty years would pass, however, before a shovel sliced into the ground in either place. From the waterfront in Cobourg, the C&P began building northward along the banks of Cobourg Brook to Harwood on Rice Lake in 1853. (The rice beds which gave the early aboriginal inhabitants a food source, and the lake its name, were submerged when the lake level was raised by a control dam built during construction of the Trent Canal.)

Now, to circumvent the lake would have meant building a long detour, so the railway builders bridged it. The strange structure extended for three kilometres and included a causeway form Harwood to Tick Island. Between there and the north shore were 33 eighty-foot truss spans that contained a 120-foot swing bridge to allow steamers to pass. From Hiawatha the line continued to Peterborough (actually into Ashburnham, the name given to the settlement on the east bank of the Otonabee River at Peterborough), and later to Chemong Lake.

But no sooner was the bridge completed in 1853 than the trouble began. The following spring a southeast wind hurled the ice against the flimsy structure, tearing it to pieces. Repairs were made and trains rumbled once more over the causeway; but each spring the pattern was repeated. By 1860 the trestle had become so rickety that it forced the Prince of Wales to abort his tour of the railway — the bridge had become too dangerous for royalty to cross.

By 1866 the company had shifted its attention to the iron mines at Blairton, east of Rice Lake, and gave up the unpredictable crossing. It even changed its name, becoming the Cobourg Peterborough and Marmora Railway. The CPM added a connection between the Trent River, near the east end of Rice Lake, and Blairton, and replaced the causeway with steamers. Meanwhile, the newly built Grand Junction Railway had slipped around Rice Lake from the east, taking over the CPM's former point of entry into Peterborough.

All Aboard

This short route leads from Cobourg, one of Ontario's best preserved 19th century towns, to the shady shores of Rice Lake, and on to another city with plenty of history, Peterborough. The side trip from Trent River, meanwhile, leads to one of Ontario's oldest ghost towns. Although the railway vestiges are relatively few, their sheer interest value alone more than compensates.

In Cobourg the line led from its station and warehouses on the harbour, north up Springer Street crossing the CPR and CNR tracks (although the CPR was many years in the future when the C&P was under con-

The Harwood station was moved to Roseneath where it found a new home as a Loyal Orange lodge.

struction, and the Grand Trunk was then barely under construction). New development on the Cobourg waterfront has removed all traces of the railway, although here and there the rails peep through the asphalt on Springer Street. The CNR crossing is still clearly visible and, until the late 1980s, contained a short storage track.

The former C&P station still stands, moved to Stuart Street to become a house. By contrast, the Grand Trunk station, recently renovated by VIA, bears every resemblance to an elegant turn-of-the-century passenger station. Inside the long stone and brick building, VIA has restored the high ceiling and replaced the molded fibreglass seats so common in post-war stations with period wooden benches.

Before leaving Cobourg, visit Victoria College and, on the main street, Victoria Hall, also restored to its 19th century splendour. Your route then takes you north on Highway 45 to the mill town of Baltimore, with its massive 19th century wooden grist mill. You can glimpse the old railway roadbed by following County Road 74 west to Cobourg Brook. Overgrown and scarcely visible other than as a mound, this represents its condition for most of its route along the banks of the creek.

Continue north of Baltimore on Highway 45 to Harwood Road. Until you reach

Blairton, the CPM's second terminus, became a ghost town.

County Road 9 the old roadbed and the creek to which it clings remain mostly out of sight. Finally, north of County Road 9 the two merge and you can drive on the old C&P into Harwood. Somewhere south of Harwood, along the right of way, lie the long lost graves of a group of Dutch railway workers killed in the line of duty. Drive straight to the shore of the lake and park by a small public beach. Here, where the station and wharf once stood, the eroded causeway stretches out into the lake. If you're careful you can walk along it but be wary, for in parts it is only the width of a footpath and is quite steep. The station at Harwood, which stood into this century, was disassembled and moved to Roseneath on Highway 45 to be constructed as an Orange Lodge. An historic plaque in front of the Harwood community hall commemorates the ill-fated little railway.

Since there is no longer anything to carry you across the lake, you must return to County Road 9 and follow it west to Highway 28. Take it north to Peterborough County Road 2 (the Keene road) and drive the 14 kilometres to Mathers Corners. After passing the North Rice Lake Road, you are back at the right of way, here an elevated ridge. Beside the ridge on the south side of the road stands what was an old brick hotel, aligned to the railway. During the railway's brief life, the building served as a hotel and "station" for passengers transferring to stages that would carry them east or west into the then developing farmlands of Peterborough County.

From the Keene Road follow County Road 30 north to Peterborough. North of the first crossroad to the old C&P right of way, here barely visible, crosses your path.

About two kilometres farther, clearly evident, is that of the more recently abandoned Grand Junction. These two lines linked at a place called Downer Corners at the intersection of Lansdowne Street and Ashburnham Road.

The first railway to arrive in Peterborough, the C&P built its station and yards north of Hunter Street, west of Rogers Road. The space is vacant now but the station survived into the 1960s serving as a storage facility, and the CNR maintained a spur line for a few years after that. Drive north on Rogers to Hazlitt, then west to the right of way where an old railway building, likely a lunch room for crews, still stands.

When the line was extended to Chemong Lake in 1859 it crossed the Otonabee River beside Parkhill Road East. On the west side of the river turner south from Parkhill onto Elcombe. On the west side of this short crescent a cluster of railway cabins, feature in local history books, marks the location of the right of way.

Like Cobourg, Peterborough retains many historical buildings and is worth spending time in; not just to drop into the Chamber of Commerce which occupies the century old CPR station on George Street. The clock tower on the market building, now a shopping centre, has been a landmark in downtown Peterborough for as long as the CPR station has been around.

Between Peterborough and Chemong Lake, nothing remains of the right of way. Even its terminus, Chemong, about four kilometres beyond the Bridgenorth causeway, has vanished. The story of the C&P, at this time the CPM, continues 40 kilometres east of Peterborough in the riverside village of

Trent River. (You may wish to follow the old Grand Junction route to this point, the directions for which are in chapter 16.) Although the line which was abandoned in the 1870s is nearly impossible to trace, you can see it where it crosses Preneveau Road south of Highway 7 and east of Havelock; Trent River and Blairton, the two villages at either point, invite exploration.

Trent River, now primarily a resort community, occupies a pretty location on the swirling river of the same name. Blairton, the site of Canada's premier iron mine during the 1860s and 70s, is a ghost town. Ore from Blairton's "big pit" was shipped over the CPM to Trent River, from which point it was barged to Harwood and then taken once more by rail to Cobourg. Blairton was developed on a grid network of streets and at its peak a population of 500 lived in company houses, large homes, or boarding houses.

Those heady times ended in the 1870s when the ore deposits gave out. Blairton's population shrank to less than 100, and by the early years of this century a mere 25 people wandered the empty streets. By following the Blairton Road north from Highway 7 a short distance west of Marmora, you come to the abandoned streets and the cellar holes of the houses and hotels, among them a solitary worker's cabin. But much new development is occurring in the vicinity, giving the area a vitality unknown since the days of the old CPM. You can pick up the trail of the abandoned Central Ontario Railway, which is the topic of Chapter 17, by continuing west into Marmora.

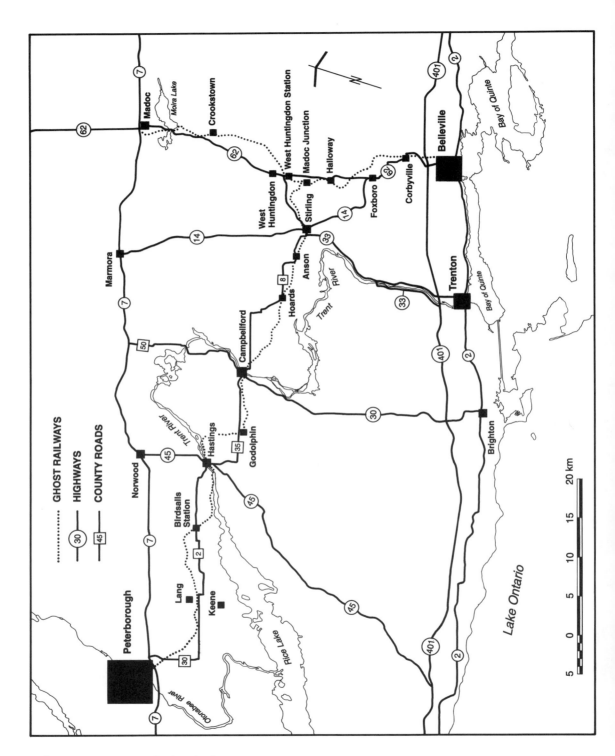

GHOST RAILWAYS

········ GHOST RAILWAYS

——— HIGHWAYS

——— COUNTY ROADS

(30) HIGHWAYS

[45] COUNTY ROADS

Peterborough

Norwood

Lang

Keene

Birdsalls Station

Hastings

Godolphin

Campbellford

Hoards

Anson

Marmora

West Huntingdon

Stirling

Foxboro

Corbyville

Halloway

Madoc Junction

West Huntingdon Station

Crookstown

Madoc

Belleville

Trenton

Brighton

Bay of Quinte

Bay of Quinte

Lake Ontario

Rice Lake

Trent River

Trent River

Moira Lake

Otonabee River

20 km

CHAPTER SIXTEEN

The Big Loop: Ontario's Grand Junction Railway

Backgrounder

Most of Ontario's early railway lines barged straight inland from a port and stopped either where the forests and farms ended or when the construction money did. But in 1852 the Grand Junction promoters proposed a different approach. They would loop a line from Belleville where it would connect with the Grand Trunk Railway around Rice Lake to Peterborough, and then back to meet the Grand Trunk again at Toronto. This configuration would give the railway two ports and an extensive hinterland of farms and forests.

But money dried up before the loop could be started and the project was shelved until 1873. By then other railway lines had penetrated the area between Peterborough and Toronto — the Nipissing, the Midland, the Whitby Port Perry and Lindsay — and so the Grand Junction went only as far as Peterborough, and even that took seven years to complete. A gold rush in Hastings captured the interest of the Grand Junction and it built a spur line to Madoc near the gold fields. Then when the Midland Railway went on a binge and acquired the Grand Junction as well as other lines be-

tween Peterborough and Toronto, the loop was at last complete, at least in terms of corporate ownership. Passengers could travel until the late 1950s and freight service lasted into the 1980s. Then the CNR, the owner since 1923, giving up as it did on most of branch lines, walked away.

All Aboard

This route, from Belleville to Peterborough, leads you through a landscape of rolling hills and rivers, of family farms, and of country towns, most of which grew because of the railway. You will find opportunities to drive or walk the right of way; you will see historic town buildings and even a couple of former stations.

Your starting point is Belleville. Despite unsightly urban sprawl on its peripheries, Belleville is a handsome and historic town. Begun as a port in the sheltered waters of the Bay of Quinte, Belleville dates to the 1790s and the arrival of the United Empire Loyalists. The Grand Trunk came to town in 1856 and gave the place an important economic boost.

New hotels and parklands have opened some of Belleville's shoreline, while its main street, dominated by its landmark town hall, has received new streetscaping. Start with the Grand Trunk station located on Station Street. This original depot was built in 1856 and has served Belleville since then. With its trademark stone arch windows and its mansard roof, the building was modernized by Via Rail. The railway offices added in the 1890s and located beside the station were demolished by CNR in the late 1980s. Next to that at Kingston,

the station is the busiest between Toronto and Montreal. Via trains call fourteen times a day on their way to and from Toronto, Montreal, and Ottawa. In front of the station, the CNR yards stretch away for a kilometre, where CNR yard engines putter back and forth assembling train units.

From Station Street drive north on Cannifton Road, Highway 37.

Despite having just departed busy Belleville, your first stop is something of a "ghost" town, Corbyville. A company town, it started in 1857 with Henry Corby's flour mill. Two years later he

The GJR's branch to Madoc was an attempt to penetrate the mining country to the north. (OA)

added a distillery which became the largest in the Canadas within just five years. It remained one of Canada's leading distilleries until operations fell silent in the early 1990s. The vats and company offices now sit empty. Many of the houses in the town-site were removed while others remain, occupied by commuters to Belleville. At first glance Corbyville does not appear to be a "railway" town; nonetheless, the location of the line was instrumental in its growth. You can still see the right of way on the east side of the town as well as the company offices, the landscaping, and the now silent industrial buildings.

From the company offices follow the river road for two kilometres to a T inter-section and turn left, crossing the bridge that brings you into Foxboro. Foxboro is a collection of old and new buildings, a one-time mill town that has gained a new life as a commuter town for Belleville. The site of the station was 1.5 kilometres east on County Road 5. The right of way embankment stretches off on the north side of the road; on the south are the remains of the bridge that carried the railway over the Moira River.

Return on County Road 5 west to Highway 62 and head north. About two kilometres north, the right of way crosses the highway and begins to snake its way through ridges of round hills that dominate the landscape. Known by geologists as drumlins,

Strollers pass the preserved Stirling station.

they were sculpted smooth by the monster glaciers that crept over Ontario more than 20,000 years ago. Forced to seek gaps between the hills, the GJR twisted north to Madoc Junction, an important point from which the gold field line branched north. Tucked between a pair of drumlins, the site today is overgrown and trackless. Despite the presence of a couple of older houses there is nothing to tell that a railway even ran here. To reach the site turn west from Highway 62 two kilometres north of the hamlet of Halloway and follow Boundary Road until it bends west. Madoc Junction lies lifeless in the bottom of the valley one half kilometre beyond.

Return to Highway 62 and continue north to follow the gold field branch. After three kilometres the right of way crosses the highway at a location that was known as West Huntington Station. The right of way then swings east of the road to cross farm fields and then enters the swamps along Rawdon Creek. You'll find it again at Crookston, on County Road 38 about 1.5 kilometres east of the highway. One kilometre south of the village the line passed under the CPR; it too has been abandoned.

From Crookston the roadbed continues through the lowlands of Rawdon Creek, skirts White Lake, and crosses Huntington Concession 11/12 at the site for Moira

The name board and a feed mill are about all that survived of Hoards' railway heritage.

Lake Station. It then hugs the cliffs that line the south shore of Moira Lake, a lake popular with fishing enthusiasts and cottagers. The right of way crosses Highway 62 at the narrows of the lake. Although the bridge has gone you can yet see the location of the abutments. Beside the highway the railway trestle over the narrows is still in place.

Madoc, the jumping off point for the gold fields, is today a small retail service town for the surrounding rural community and for highway travellers. The railway entered town 1.5 kilometres west of Highway 62. The little wooden station survived, a vandalized shell, overgrown and neglected, until 1990 when it finally was burned. (Several earlier attempts at arson had left their scars on the shell of the station.) From Madoc you can design a circle route that takes you back to Belleville by way of the Bay of Quinte route (Chapter 18) from Bannockburn 16 kilometres north. Or, you may continue north on the Central Ontario Railway (Chapter 17) from Eldorado, the heart of the gold fields, 11 kilometres north.

However, to continue following the main line of the Grand Junction, return south on Highway 62 to West Huntington Station and follow County Road 6 west to Stirling. The right of way parallels the road

Much railway memorabilia lingers beside the GJR right of way in Campbellford.

about 500 metres south of it and crosses to the north side at the outskirts of Stirling, a little known community that is well worth pausing in. A row of handsome 19th century stores and businesses face onto a tiny parkette in the centre of town in which a miniature covered bridge has been built across Rawdon Creek.

And then there's the station. One block east of the main intersection, turn north. The local community has preserved the station and repainted it. This two-storey "Van Horne" style of station was commonly used on CPR lines until the 1890s when that railway replaced most with more elaborately styled structures. The style was rarely seen on CNR or its predecessors' lines, however, and is quite peculiar to Stirling. Furthermore, the right of way remains open for strollers, cyclists, and even vehicles.

You can drive the roadbed west from Stirling to the next stop, Anson, although it may be safer to continue on County Road 6. The site of the diamond between the COR and the GJR, Anson was never more than a small collection of railway houses, and today is a scattered rural community. The crossover remains visible a few paces south of the county road along the COR roadbed. Several small bridges were needed here to cross the meandering creeks.

From Anson the GJR wanders over roll-

Even in its simplicity, the station at Keene was an attractive structure.

ing farmlands for six kilometres to the hamlet of Hoards Station; the county road follows it. Once a busy shipping point for the railway, the hamlet retains to this day a feed mill operation, an industry that owes its origin to the coming of the railway. In memory of the community's railway roots, someone has rescued the station name board and placed it on a garage.

Once more the right of way winds through the rolling drumlin fields that characterize the geology of the area. While the ownership of the roadbed is debated, the right of way remains open and is popular with local snowmobilers and all-terrain-vehicle users.

A dozen more kilometres brings both road and rail line into Campbellford. Although the station was demolished, Campbellford retains a surprising collection of historic structures. Several mill buildings line the east bank of the Trent River, while on the west side along the right of way, an ancient and abandoned feed mill has survived, beside it the former freight station. The mill and freight shed are south of Highway 30 at the corner of Alma and Simpson Streets. Sadly, despite their high historic value, some of these structures appear to have survived more because the owners haven't yet torn them down, than through any conscious effort to preserve them.

The Trent Canal follows the river through Campbellford; much of the west bank of the river is parkland from which you can watch sleek yachts and small run-abouts jostle for space in the cramped canal locks.

Now take Highway 30 west from Campbellford for 2.5 kilometres, continuing west on County Road 15. For the next 12

kilometres the road and rail line pass through more rolling farmlands. The roadbed lies to the south of the road until the halfway point where it suddenly turns sharply north near what was once a sideing named "Godolphin." Reaching the shore of the Trent River, the right of way follows the river westward into Hastings. County Road 15 enters from the south.

Hastings too retains some railway relics. On the east side of the highway you will see the old grain elevator, and to the west, the station site. Smaller than that at Stirling, the Hastings depot was a simple design, a single storey with a gable above the bay. Following its original closure it re-opened as an antique store but has since burned down.

Highway 45 cuts through Hastings. Follow it over the bridge to the centre of the village and take County Road 2 (the Keene Road) west. For the next six kilometres the line follows the bank of the Trent River before cutting back inland to Birdsalls Station. The road, meanwhile, continues through a landscape much like that you have been following: field and pasture on the rolling whale-back hills.

A hotel and small community grew up around Birdsalls Station, named after a rural community three kilometres to the south. The station stood on the south side of high bridge that carries the road over the rail line, and was on the west side of the track. The old hotel still survives and remains open as a store.

Continue driving west for seven kilometres and then turn north onto the road between Otonabee Concessions 4 and 5, then turn left again. This brings you to the Indian River and a community known as Keene Station. Between Birdsalls and

Keene Stations the line itself winds between the drumlins, a configuration that makes the former railway route two kilometres longer than the road. Only a siding named Blezard lay between the two station sites. Throughout this section the right of way appears open, although at this writing the ultimate ownership remains undecided and the entire line may well be closed and sold.

While in the area, plan to visit the preserved pioneer village at Lang, north of the village of Keene. Cabins, churches, and mills built by the area's early settlers have been preserved and moved here. But strangely absent are railway stations and the story of the role that the old Grand Junction Railway played in the history of the area.

The last stop for the GJR was Peterborough. While the diamond between the GJR and the C&P cannot be discerned, you can easily see the remains of the bridges that carried the Grand Junction over the Otonabee and on into Peterborough: they are just north of the Lansdowne Street bridge. The Grand Junction was ultimately absorbed by the Midland Railway and then by the Grand Trunk. The brick station that served until the 1960s was a Grand Trunk structure. It stood south of Hunter Street and was torn down to make way for an apartment complex.

GJR passengers disembarked at the Grand Trunk's beautiful Peterborough station, demolished to make way for a an apartment building. (MTL)

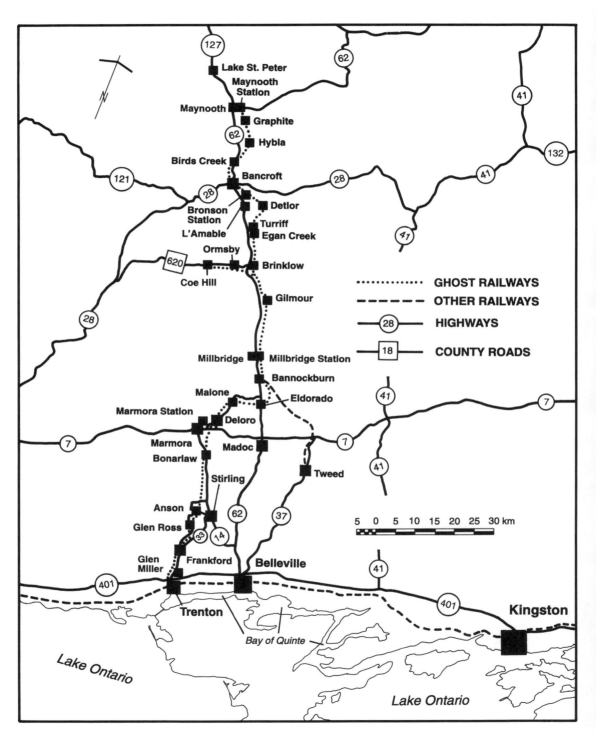

CHAPTER SEVENTEEN

The Central Ontario Railway: Into the Hills of Gold

Backgrounder

At 117 miles (from Trenton to north of Maynooth), the Central Ontario Railway (COR) represents one of the longest ghost railways in Ontario. Along it the explorer will find trails, stations and, in the towns and villages that line it, much of the mining and pioneer lore that colours the story of the line itself.

Begun in 1873, the line was ultimately intended to link with the legendary Booth railway near Whitney. While the rails did succeed in penetrating a rocky wilderness of forest and swamp., it fell short of Booth's line by mere miles. While the rails ended at Wallace, the real terminus was at Maynooth to the south. Here the railway had yards, turntables, and its largest station.

The story begins in the County of Prince Edward with completion of a line between Picton (although Long Point was originally to have been the port and termi-nus) and Trenton Junction, its link with the Grand Trunk just jorth of Trenton. But the glitter of the gold rush to the hills north of Trenton and Belleville in 1866 danced in the eyes of the railway builders. Determined

to be first to the gold fields, builders of the rival Grand Junction Railway hurried a line that led from Belleville northwest to Peterborough, opening it in 1879. A branch led northward from Madoc Junction to the ill-fated goldfields of Eldorado. Eventually, though, it was a mineral more practical than gold that convinced the builders of the COR to look north: iron. In 1882 con-struction began.

The first destination was Coe Hill, centre of the earliest iron discoveries. Later, as prospectors stumbled through the hills south of Bancroft, unearthing more iron, the line followed: finally, in 1900, it reached Bancroft. Then in 1909 the Canadian Northern Railway of MacKenzie and Mann laid its Toronto and Ottawa main line through Trenton, adding to their empire the Central Ontario Railway. The COR replaced Trenton's wooden station with a grand three-story building and, at the north end, extended the line to Maynooth. It met the Irondale Bancroft and Ottawa (IBO) at Birds Creek, north of Bancroft, where another large station was added. Along the route branch lines struck off toward the busy mine camps.

Gradually the mines were depleted and the mine branches closed: that to Cordova Mines in 1941, to Bessemer and Lake St. Peter in 1965, and to Coe Hill in 1966; the mines themselves had closed long before.

And as the CNR tired of running short lines it considered to be unprofitable, it chopped back the main line of the COR piece by piece. That north of Marmora went in 1982, while the link from Trenton to Marmora was abandoned in 1986.

All Aboard

Your route for the COR begins at Trenton Junction. Here on Old Wooler Road, west of Trenton Street, the COR passes beneath the main CNR line. The rails here were among the last to be lifted. While the large station that the Grand Trunk built to serve the location has long been replaced by what resembles a bus shelter, the COR's one time boarding house still stands on the north side of the road, beside the track.

North to Frankford the right of way is out of sight from the road, Highway 33. Nevertheless, you can hike it or snowmobile along it. The historic paper mill village of Glen Miller was served by the line and still contains historic industrial structures including the mill buildings and offices.

A short distance north, behind a limestone mesa at the back of the De Jong store, the right of way passes the unusual Glen Miller boulder. You can hike along the roadbed south from the first road north of the store to the boulder. Larger than a house, this glacial erratic is located to the south of the right of way. A trail leads up the embankment past a bridge over a small creek.

A short distance north you will encounter one of the stranger sites of the route: the partly vanished village of Batawa. Constructed in 1939 as the headquarters for the Thomas Bata shoe empire, it stood as a company town. However all of the original company houses have been removed, leaving a strange pattern of roads, sidewalks and driveways. In the original townsite the only buildings to have survived are a church, a school, and a library. You can see the vanished village by following Thomas Bata Blvd. west from the highway.

Until 1993 the station at Frankford, the next stop on the line, rested on its original site three blocks west of the highway and was used as a Lions Club meeting hall. It now sits in the village of Stockdale, a few kilometres to the west. At Frankford, you "leave" Highway 33. More accurately, it leaves you and crosses the Trent River; you continue straight north. Again the line follows the river, out of view of the road, until both road and rail reach Glen Ross.

Here you will find a 400-foot bridge over the Trent River, and another of the route's stranger sights, sitting high and dry on the south bank of the Trent Canal: a disused swing bridge. Built in 1905, the bridge served the railway until the rails were lifted in the 1980s.

Once known as "Chisholm's," Glen Ross was the north side of the swing bridge and replaced the original station on the south shore in about 1913.

From Glen Ross to Lake St. Peter, the right of way is now known as the Hastings Heritage Trail, a multi-use recreational route. From the Trent to Bonarlaw, the line winds through field and swamp. From the south side of County Road 8, three kilometres west of

Stirling, you can drive over the right of way through a field to Anson Junction, the COR's intersection with the Grand Junction. You can trace the diamond, now surrounded by pasture, the two switching points, and you can even drive east on the GJR right of way up to the station in Stirling, a station that has survived to this day. While the station at Anson itself was on the north side of County Road 8, no settlement of any size developed here due to the proximity of Stirling.

If driving, continue north from Anson for two kilometres and then turn east to Highway 14, which leads north into Marmora. The right of way parallels the road for about one kilometre to the west. At the intersection of County Road 36 you pass through the hamlet of Springbrook. Quiet now, in days of rail it could boast saw, grist, and shingle mills as well as a cheese factory.

Four kilometres north the COR intersected the Ontario and Quebec Railway, now part of CPR's holdings, at Bonarlaw, although there was little in the way of a set-

The abandoned open pit mine at Marmora was once served by the COR.

tlement here. Indeed, the large CPR station which served both lines stood 500 metres away surrounded by fields. Three kilometres north of the CPR, the COR right of way crosses the highway and swings northeast to the imposing remains of the Marmora iron mines. Until it closed in the 1970s, the Bethlehem Steel Company stripped out twenty million tons of limestone for shipment down the COR and across to the U.S. via the port at Picton. One of southern Ontario's most imposing mine sites, the huge open pit of the Marmora iron mines, or the "big hole" as it is called locally, is slowly filling with water. You can view it safely from behind a chain-

link fence by driving east on Highway 7 from Marmora for two kilometres and then turning south on the old mine road. Another point of interest for budding geologists is that Marmora is Italian for "marble." Rock hunters might want to haul out their rock hunting guides to visit some the area's abandoned marble quarries.

While the COR main line passed east of Marmora, a short branch line ran straight through the town along the east bank of the Crowe River and on to serve the then bustling mining town of Cordova. On that long abandoned right of way in the centre of Marmora, you will find the COR's Marmora station. It is, however, some distance

A large brick hotel is all that survives in the remote ghost hamlet of Millbridge Station.

from home for the station, which was originally located seven kilometres east of the town. With the abandonment of the COR, the building, then used only for storage, was moved into town, repainted and reopened as a tourist information centre. Its style is COR station architecture at its simplest. Single-storey with a simple roofline, the style was repeated at every location on the COR between Picton and Coe Hill. Even the original Trenton station was nothing more than an elongated version of it.

Although there remains little other than a few homes, you can drive to the site of Marmora Station by turning north onto the Deloro Road, County Road 11, three kilometres east of the mine road. As the road swings right toward Deloro, the dirt road to the station site is to the left. From Marmora Station a branch line led the three kilometres into Deloro where, until the early 1960s, the Deloro Mining and Reduction Company operated a silver refinery. Smaller and quieter than Marmora, Deloro still retains much of its flavour as a mining town, although all the refinery buildings and company houses were removed after the operation closed. On the east side of the main street look for the unmistakable shape of a COR railway station that was relocated from Bannockburn. Unfortunately, an addition on the front has enclosed the bay window portion.

Continue north from Deloro. This twisting dirt road leads you to a scattered collection of dwellings that make up Malone, once the site of a sawmill and a cordwood supply depot. (Because of the seemingly endless supply of timber, the COR locomotives were later than those on other rail lines in switching to coal as a source of fuel.) The right of way crosses the road about one kilometre further on the west side of the Moira River bridge, and crossed the river right beside the road.

The road takes you to Highway 62 at a hamlet called Fox Corners. Turn south and drive two kilometres to Eldorado, a one-time boom town and site of Ontario's 1866 gold rush. Once the centre of a community that had more than eighty houses, Eldorado still contains a number of gold rush landmarks. Among them, along the highway, are three of the gold rush hotels. But once the heady rush subsided amidst rumours of fraud, many of Eldorado's buildings were abandoned. Look on the west side of the road for the historical marker that sums up this golden burst bubble. The brick building beside it is one of the old hotels, and at the end of the side street on which it sits you will come to the right of way and the station platform.

Return north on Highway 62 to Bannockburn, less than five kilometres beyond Fox Corners. The chapter on the BQ line tells you to look for the roofless engine house and station platform from this line; however, of the COR you will find only the right of way, now a dirt road. About six kilometres further, the Stoney Settlement Road leads east to Millbridge Station. The parent village, Millbridge, is to the west, and both are ghost towns. Everything at the station has gone, save what is one of the larger buildings on this route, the former Hogan's hotel. Now a house, this two-storey brick building still sports its hotel sign, hand-painted a century ago.

Millbridge itself is older. A stopping place and mill site on the Hastings Road, it prospered briefly and then, as the settlers along the road fled their failing farms, it declined. Most of its original houses and stores have long since burned down or been demolished.

But it wasn't country living that drew settlers to the Hastings Road nearly a century and a half ago; it was free land. One of the first of 25 colonization roads, it was part of a government scheme to lure settlers to this rocky wilderness with a promise of free land and rich crops. Most have labelled it a "scam" for it was little more than a ploy to provide local lumber interests with men, horses, and food supplies close at hand. When the lumber companies had razed the forests they left behind thousands of weary pioneers, many of them starving, but most without the vital off-farm jobs in the lumber camps. Most of the colonization roads were quickly abandoned leaving behind empty farms and ghost towns.

Here the Hastings Road and the COR, both abandoned, parallel each other and each offers it owns ghosts. About 15 kilometres from Stoney Settlement Road, the Weslemkoon Road leads east for two kilometres to Gilmour. This still active community once had a large sawmill, a small station, and a hotel. Of the three only the hotel, a large brick structure that today offers bed and breakfast, has survived. Meanwhile, the Hastings Road is a tortuous dry weather road which you can reach by following Steenburg Lake Road eight kilometres from Highway 62. Here the old Hastings Road leads past ghost communities like Glanmire, with its church steps and cemetery, and Murphy's Corners, once a stopping place for travellers.

Return to Highway 62 and continue north. At County Road 620 drive west to Coe Hill. Once the site of several promising iron and gold prospects, Coe Hill was the original destination for the COR railway builders. When the mines closed the town settled down and became a service centre for the farms that were hacked out of the rugged hills. Today, Coe Hill is still very much alive and has another of the COR's few original stations, preserved in the community fair grounds.

Back on Highway 62, drive north towards Bancroft. Just south of Bancroft, the Detlor Road leads east 5.5 kilometres to Detlor, the site of the L'Amable station. Demolished long ago, it was decidedly larger than those further south and resembled in style the station still standing in Bancroft. Where it stood there are still a few older homes. A short distance south of the station grounds, the Bessemer Mine Railway ran easterly to the Bessemer and Childes iron mines. Long abandoned, neither they, nor the right of way, offer up any vestiges.

Bancroft, however, is a place well worth lingering in. Its wide western-style main street still sports a few of the boom town buildings, such as the Bancroft Hotel, from its early mining days. Its current claim to fame is as the rock hound capital of North America. Every August rock hounds gather for the annual "Gemboree," a swap session and gambit into the hills in search of quartz, amazonite, sodalite or even feldspar, semi-precious stones suitable for rock tumbling and jewellery making.

But it also has its old station. More reflective of the larger and more elaborate stations that the Canadian Northern Railway lavished on the COR after it took it over, the depot contains a second-floor dormer and a freight shed. The station also contains a mining museum, an art gallery, and a number of community facilities. Simply follow the directional arrows from the main street. And with its restaurants and motels, Bancroft is a place you can pause in for a meal or an overnight stay.

Besides its rock hounding, the rugged hills around Bancroft still retain a hardy pioneer landscape with farms that have defied harsh conditions to cling to life. Mountain communities with names like Maxwell Settlement, Vardy Settlement, and Monteagle Valley are surrounded by some of southern Ontario's most rugged mountain scenery.

About four kilometres north of downtown Bancroft, Highway 62 passes York River, the site of the junction of the COR and the IBO. Between here and Maynooth were only three other station locations, Birds Creek, Hybla, and Graphite.

At the time of this writing Maynooth Station still had the largest station on the line. A massive two-storey building of concrete, the station sits two kilometres east of Maynooth on Maynooth Station Road. While the second floor contained spacious accommodation for the agent and his family, and likely some office space as well, the downstairs could boast a restaurant. Sadly, the site is overgrown, and the building gutted and vandalized. The line itself struggled only about twenty kilometres further on, ending at Wallace, well short of the terminus that its early builders had envisioned at Whitney.

The grand terminus at Maynooth Station continues to resist vandals' efforts to destroy it.

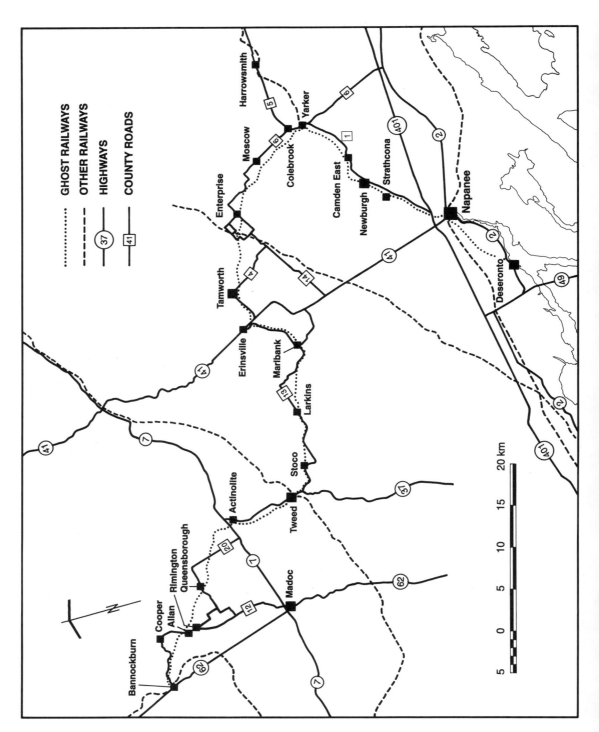

CHAPTER EIGHTEEN

The Bay of Quinte Railway: Rathbun's Road

Backgrounder

The Bay of Quinte railway (BQ), despite its almost magical story and numerous relics, is little more than a footnote in the history of the legendary company that built it.

It's a route that you can trace, sometimes drive over, past intriguing old stations still on site, bridges, and even turntables and engine houses. Many relics of the BQ have survived the lifting of the rails more than a half century ago. And there are also mill towns and country landscapes that have been spared the modern blights of highway malls and urban sprawl.

It all began with Edward Rathbun. One of those ambitious entrepreneurs spawned by the 19th century, Rathbun founded what would become one of the largest and most diversified industrial empires in 19th century Canada. From its large mills in Deseronto on the northeastern shores of Lake Ontario, the Rathbun company expanded in all directions. Its fleets carried lumber and other cargo southward to Oswego, its sister port on the New York side of Lake Ontario, while its trains moved cargo east and west along the Grand Trunk. To the

north lay the vast Rathbun timber limits and the Bay of Quinte Railway.

Like much of the Rathbun empire the railway began as a mishmash of existing short lines and unused charters. After building his own link from Deseronto a short distance to the Grand Trunk's main line west of Napanee, Rathbun then purchased the Napanee Tamworth and Quebec line, a railway that led northward from Napanee. He then extended the line northwest to Tweed and later Bannockburn, as well as northeast to Sydenham. This gave the company the all-important access to its timber limits. By 1903 the network of railway tracks had become known as the Bay of Quinte Railway.

The railway gained its revenue from more than just Rathbun's timber ventures. A marble quarry at Actinolite, a cement plant at Marlbank, and a pyrite mine at Queensborough all contributed to the BQ's profits. In 1910 the expanding Canadian Northern Railway added the BQ to its national inventory of undervalued lines. The CNo, however, was less interested in the timber, mines, and quarries, than it was in completing a main line from Toronto to Ottawa. The BQ was a valuable link in that route.

Neglected by the new owners, the cement plant, the mines, and the mills closed one by one; by 1930 only one train operated north of Tweed each week. To no-one's surprise the section between Tweed and Bannockburn was abandoned in 1935 and that from Tweed to Yarker in 1941. The CNR continued train service along the section from Napanee to Yarker and beyond to Smiths Falls until 1986.

All Aboard

The route begins in Deseronto. Sadly, despite the legacy of the Rathbuns and of the railway on the town, nothing survives to commemorate this formative period in the town's history. Tracks, station, mills, and wharfs have all gone, with little in their place except potholed roads and nondescript storage facilities. A few main street buildings are of historic note, however: these include the stone town hall in the centre of the village and the Mohawk chapel to the west.

ABOVE: The main street of Deseronto displays an historic prosperity that owes its origin to the enterprise and railway that the Rathbuns built. FACING PAGE: Newburgh's station (top) and railway hotel (bottom) survive far from the more recent right of way that was built through town.

Nonetheless, Napanee does retain one relic of early railway days: a railway station built by the Grand Trunk in 1856. One of Canada's oldest, it is still a stop for Via's corridor trains between Toronto and Montreal and Toronto and Ottawa. West of the little station lay the junction of the BQ and GTR, a link that is still visible and that replaced the first junction point. East of the station the BQ's northern branch still operated to the mills at Strathcona until around 1990.

From Napanee the BQ follows the scenic valley of the Napanee River to Yarker. Take County Road 1 from Napanee. About 7 km after crossing Highway 401 you arrive in Strathcona. Here, by the overgrown right of way, you will see the much expanded paper mill, and to the north of the track the small but historic core of the one-time mill village.

Three more kilometres leads you to the village of Newburgh. A mill town on the river since 1824, the place lost most of its buildings to fire in 1887, but it still contains

You can drive on the BQ right way right past the old platform of the former Stoco station, shown here in its railway days. (LCM)

many old stone buildings, including the Newburgh Academy on the north end of town, some old stone stores, and the station. However, you won't find it on the right of way, at least not on the later, more visible right of way. In the early days the track ran closer to the river, but frequent flooding forced its relocation about one kilometre north. By following Grove Street east from the main street you will come to the original station built in the distinctive BQ design, and still on its original site (the later station on the relocated line was demolished). Across from it the stone railway hotel is a private home, as is the station; both can be viewed without trespassing.

Less than four kilometres further on, County Road 1 leads into Camden East. With historic stores and hotels on the main intersections, it retains at least part of a pioneer legacy which dates to 1818, when it was established as a mill village named Clark's Mills. It has retained none of its railway legacy, however, and the right of way, abandoned for just eight years, has become a dry weather road. Although unrelated to the railway, look for the little ghost town of Thompson Mills. Marked by the shell of

Ruins in the woods are that remain of the Marlbank cement works that looked like this while operating. (LCM)

a stone mill in a field on the north side of the road as you enter Camden East, it once contained a store and several mill workers' houses.

Continue for seven kilometres from Camden East to County Road 6 and the scenic riverside community of Yarker. Nestled around the falls on the river that provided the power for its early mills as early as 1840, the village still exudes a 19th century aura, although most of its stores are now closed or are used only as residences.

From Yarker the original BQ line headed northwest. But when the CNo acquired the line it extended the route that led northeasterly to Ottawa. Yarker was the point where the two branches divided. The original BQ line was finally abandoned in 1941 while the route to Smiths Falls lasted another 45 years. The station site can be found by crossing the river and following the side road up the hill. On the west side of the road the right of way is a dry weather road, on the east an overgrown path. The railway bridge, however, still spans the river, but the one you see was a replacement for the original, whose remains lie just beyond.

County Road 6 continues to Colebrook and then northwestward through Moscow. The station and right of way which were located about 1.5 kilometres west of the vil-

The Queensborough station is now a private home, as are many on this line.

lage have disappeared beneath ploughed fields. County Road 6 carries on through field and swamp for another 12 kilometres to County Road 14 and Enterprise about two kilometres to the west. While a number of historic stores and houses have survived from the town's railway heyday, the station has not.

West of Enterprise the BQ crossed the still active Ottawa branch of the CPR. You can see those abutments by driving north from the main intersection in Enterprise for about one kilometre and turning left onto the first side road. After about two kilometres the road bends north and crosses the

CPR. The stone abutments lie about 500 metres west of the road.

Return to County Road 14 and drive west to County Road 4 and follow it north to Tamworth. From here to Bannockburn your route follows the right of way and passes old stations that have changed little since the lifting of rail in the 1940s. Originally known as Wheeler's Mills, after an early mill owner from Vermont, Tamworth was settled by refugees of the Irish potato famine, and had become a busy spot even before the railway arrived. To see the station in Tamworth, turn left from County Road 4 just after the bridge. A typical BQ two-storey structure, similar to that in New-

The forest hides the massive shell of the Bannockburn BQ engine house.

burgh, it sits on the east side of the road, with the freight shed and platform still in place. It too is a private home.

From Tamworth take County Road 4 west to Highway 41. Follow it north to Erinsville. After less than one half kilometre look for the now closed Lakeview Hotel. This is the former railway hotel for the village, and beside it sits the station, most recently a storage facility for the provincial highway ministry. Pause by Beaver Lake beside the station and enjoy a picnic in the small park.

A short distance north is the centre of Erinsville village where you turn west onto County Road 12 to take you to Marlbank. This picturesque village of 19th century homes is one of the Rathbun company's cement villages. Close to today's village, on the shores of Marl Lake, Rathbun built extensive cement works that included a factory and a workers' village. These closed in 1908 when the Canada Portland Cement Company took over and shut down most of Ontario's smaller cement factories. But the station still stands at the south end of the village at the junction of County Roads 12 and 13. It is another private home and sits on the east side of the road; it replicates the style found in Tamworth and Newburgh.

As you turn onto County Road 13 west, you enter the train engineer's cabin ready to ride the right of way itself. About one kilometre west on the south side of the road you pass the ruins of the cement plant, massive stoneworks now overtaken by the forest. Then much of County Road 13 follows the gentle curves and grades that were the BQ railway. Just as it did the BQ engineers, the roadbed leads you right to the platform of yet another station, which the

name board announces as Stoco. It too is in the BQ style, and it too is a private home.

Continue west to Highway 37 which leads north into the scenic lakeside village of Tweed. Tweed marks the location of the crossing between the CPR and the BQ. The latter added a small engine house and yards and a station that was a simpler, single-storey structure. It stood just a block east of the main street across the tracks from the CPR station. While the BQ station is gone, that of the CPR, a "Van Horne" style, survives as a lumber office.

Tweed also claims to have North America's smallest jail. Although it hasn't housed a miscreant since the 1930s, its 4.8 by 6 metre measurements make the stone building a popular attraction. The largest community on this route, Tweed is a good location to rest from exploring, have a picnic, a meal, or even stay overnight in the delightfully located Park Place Motel overlooking Stoco Lake.

From Tweed the line followed the bank of the Skootamata River northward to Actinolite; the highway follows suit. East of the highway in Actinolite you will find a marble church and community hall, while to the west and across the river the right of way and station grounds. Both, however, have been largely obliterated by a quarry operation.

To return to the line, drive west from Actinolite along Highway 7 for three kilometres to County Road 20 and follow it north for ten kilometres to Queensborough. This once busy mill town and railway point is today a quiet backwater, off the beaten track but possessing many century-old wooden hotels and stores and the remains of the mill.

But there's also a station. To view it, turn left immediately after you cross the river, and then left again for about one kilometre. The station, now a home, is set back from the road on the west. The narrow sidewalk leading to it is in fact the platform. While the owners discourage visitors, the building is easily visible from the road.

From Queensborough continue on County Road 20 westerly to its T intersection with County Road 12 and turn north. Eight kilometres leads you to the site of the station known as Allan. Although there was no village at this site, the station served the nearby settlements of Rimington and Cooper. If the grass and shrubs are not too tall, you may yet see the station platform on the west side of the road.

At Cooper, a crossroads three kilometres further on (there is a community centre on the northeast corner), turn west and follow Cooper Road to Bannockburn. It was here that the BQ crossed yet another rail line, that of the Central Ontario Railway, and abruptly ended. As you enter the village on the Cooper Road, you will cross the Central Ontario Railway right of way, now an unmaintained dirt road; to the north is the "diamond" where the BQ and the COR crossed.

If you continue a short distance north on Highway 62, you will see to the west a small side road leading to a string of smaller homes. From that road a trail follows the BQ roadbed west through the woods to the largest of the BQ ruins, the former two-stall engine house. If the bush is not in its full summer density, you can find nearby the walls of the turntable and the foundations of the station.

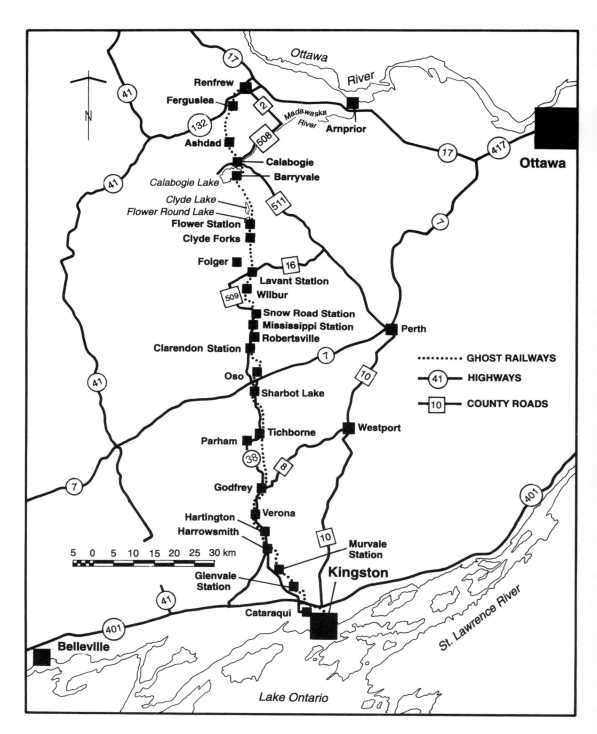

CHAPTER NINETEEN

The Kingston and Pembroke Railway: the Kick and Push Trail

Backgrounder

Of all Ontario's ghost railways, the Kingston and Pembroke provides rail fans with their closest look at the past. You can play "engineer" and drive the original roadbed, only slightly altered, a distance of 30 kilometres, from Snow Road to Calabogie, through a region of scenic lakeside vistas and wide silent marshlands.

Like many of Ontario's ghost railways, the K&P was built as a resource railway. Its promoters, Kingston ship builder C.F. Guildersleeve, C.V. Price, and the wealthy Flower family of New York, were drawn by the lustre of iron deposits and the ubiquitous timber stands. To reach them, they surveyed a railway that would lead north from Kingston and be the first railway to reach the village of Pembroke on the Ottawa River, already a vibrant mill town.

Finally, in 1884, fully 12 years after its charter was granted, the line was finished. Although it earned profits of $22,000 in its first year alone, it lost the race to Pembroke. The Canada Central Railway, which would shortly become the Canadian Pacific, got there first and the K&P had to settle for a terminus at Renfrew.

The optimism soon faded even further. The timber quickly began to run out, the iron deposits were smaller than originally thought, and the line began to lose money. One by one the railway's boosters bailed out: the Gildersleeves, the Flowers, the Prices, and even the latecomer Folgers. Finally, in 1910, the CPR took over the little line and incorporated it into its monster network as a feeder line. The corporation released most of the K&P station agents and replaced them with caretaker agents.

The nature of the line changed too. As the little lakes north of Kingston attracted more and more summer cottagers, the K&P bustled with happy holidayers. In the pre-car era the only way north to resorts like Sharbot Lake, Snow Road, Flower Station, and Calabogie was the little railway. Riders found the twists and grades so slow that they took to naming the railway the "Kick and Push," a nickname that has long outlived the line's demise.

Sawmills, farms, and a marble mine continued to provide the railway with a dwindling supply of freight. But by 1963 the line north of Snow Road was abandoned. The sawmill and marble quarry here kept the line open until 1970 when all trackage north of Tichborne was lifted. Finally, by 1986, the entire line had become another of Ontario's ghost railways. However, it is one that offers a variety of experiences for the railway chaser. Preserved steam locomotives, old stations, scenery, ghost towns, fishing from a causeway, and even the opportunity to drive the right of way, all these await the eager explorer.

All Aboard

Kingston offers a treasure trove for any history buff, from the well-known bastion of Fort Henry to the lesser known but equally historic abandoned shipbuilders' village on Garden Island. Churches, stores, and government offices built from local limestone all give the place a feel of history that few other cities in Ontario can match.

In the centre of it all is the stone K&P railway station. With its steam engine "The Spirit of Sir John A." parked in front, it is hard to miss. Now a visitors' information centre, it sits in the middle of Confederation Park on the waterfront opposite the spectacular domed city hall. Built in 1884, it replaced a smaller temporary station that sat at the corner of Ontario Street and Place d'Armes. It probably attracts more visitors today than it did as a station when it witnessed royal tours, whistle stopping politicians, and even the funeral train of Sir John A. MacDonald.

Through Kingston itself few parts of the right of way remain visible. It merged with

The K&P's Kingston station, here still in railway service, is now the centrepiece of the city's waterfront park, complete with an old steam engine.

and then crossed the CNR line west of the former GT "outer" station on Montreal Street, and then crossed Sydenham Road beside Highway 401, the site of the "Cataraqui" station. Between the Sydenham Road and Highway 38, Highway 401 still crosses over the right of way on a bridge.

Highway 38 north is the route to follow for most of this journey. The stations that served Glenvale, seven kilometres from the 401 ramp, and Murvale, about five kilometres beyond that, were well to the east of these hamlets. Other than a few railway era homes, nothing remains at these sites.

There is, however, something to see at Harrowsmith. Through this village, itself an interesting collection of 19th century buildings, the Canadian Northern Railway and the K&P shared a right of way and a station. While the rails have been lifted, you can easily see the right of way as you enter from the south. To find the station grounds, however, you must turn left onto Ottawa Street and drive a few metres back to the roadbed. On the east side of the road you may yet discern the asphalt platform of the old station. And if you look to the south of the right of way you will see the station itself, a long white building with a bell-cast roof that now serves as a private dwelling.

The right of way then parallels the highway north from Harrowsmith, through Hartington, where little more than a trail marks the site of the railway and its station. (The Holleford meteor crater lies seven kilometres northeast of the village and is well worth the side trip.) Originally known as Buzztown (nobody knows why), Verona possesses a most peculiar shape: the entire village stretches along the highway. The railway ran behind the stores on the west side of the street and, other than vacant lots, has left no legacy.

At Godfrey, eight kilometres north of Verona, the railway ventures close to the road once again. The little hamlet's only claim to fame today is its flea market; but it also has one of the most interesting buildings on the route. Anticipating that Godfrey might become a major railway town — after all the Glendower Iron Mines were producing just a few miles to the east — investors built a large store by the tracks with a two-storey ornate house attached.

After the mines closed, the boom evaporated and Godfrey remained a hamlet. The branch line to the long vanished Glendower mines is today marked only by an old railway storage building east of the store. The store itself survives. The K&P roadbed closely follows the east side of the highway through Godfrey and remains visible as a trail.

As Highway 38 continues north, the views of the K&P are lost in the rocky ridges and marshes that typify this region of Ontario. At Parham you will encounter an active railway line, the CPR's main line from Toronto to Montreal. The K&P returns at Tichborne, four kilometres east of Parham.

Tichborne was the K&P's junction with the CPR's main line, and boasted a large station. The building stood on the east side of the highway with a platform that extended around to the K&P tracks. In its place today is a yellow aluminum cabin for maintenance crews. The abandoned K&P roadbed behind it is now a cinder potholed lane and briefly parallels the highway through the village. Tichborne marks the K&P's last stand for it was to this point that the last section of the K&P remained in place until 1986.

The roadbed follows Highway 38 much of the way to Sharbot Lake, yet another important junction. The K&P reached this lakeside location in 1876, just four years ahead of the Ontario and Quebec railway then under construction from Toronto to Ottawa.

A popular tourist resort now as then, the community contains a few vestiges of its railway legacy. The site of the railway station, with the platform still evident, are beside a park on the lake. Follow Elizabeth Street west from the highway. The two

The station platform in Sharbot Lake was used by trains of both the K&P and the Ontario and Quebec line, both later owned by the CPR. (QA)

lines joined to cross the lake on a causeway that is visible on the west side of the highway as you enter town from the south. North of the station the lines separated with the Quebec and Ontario Railway (the Q&O) continuing east to Ottawa (it is now a public trail) and the K&P winding its way northward, entering ever deeper into the hill country that earned the line its nickname the "Kick and Push."

To continue, travel west from the intersection of Highway 38 with Highway 7 at Sharbot Lake. After a little more than one kilometre you will cross over the abandoned line. Turn north onto Route 509 and drive to Bell Line Road which leads you

two kilometres east to the site of Oso Station. Three frame buildings date from railway days and the right of way has become a snowmobile trail.

Less than eight kilometres north of Bell Line Road you will come to Clarendon, something of a ghost town and a place whose appearance has changed little since the days of rail. While the former hotel was removed in recent years, the former store has survived, as has the station, the only one other than that in Kingston to have survived on site. Built by the CPR in 1917 in one of its "western" plan styles, it still has the name board, the original paint scheme, and the railway platform. It replaced the

Old homes cluster around the site of the Oso Station.

original ramshackle board and batten K&P depot that had burned down.

Robertsville, on the Robertsville Road about three kilometres north of Clarendon, is another of the K&P ghost towns. Once the site of an iron mine, a boarding house, and two dozen miners' cabins, the only survivor is a solitary house and cemetery. Cellar holes, long overgrown linger in the field behind the house and along the former spur line to the mine, while opposite the house, on a hill overlooking the road, lies the small cemetery that once served this vanished village.

Just three kilometres further brings you to the next stop on the K&P, Mississippi

Station. Until the Mississippi River itself was bridged, the place was the railway's northern terminus. Its small station and hotel are gone now, but you can still view the roadbed on the east side of the road as well as a number of houses and old stores that date from those early days.

Go three kilometres across the less than mighty Mississippi, and you will reach what was one of the busiest (and today one of the prettiest) villages on the line, Snow Road Station. Its historic frame homes, its church and community hall all seem to blend, as in a picture postcard, with the woodlands and rolling fields that engulf it. The site of the station and store lie down a

The Clarendon station was the last on the line outside of Kingston.

side street that leads north from the highway near Buttermilk Falls. Here a large sawmill operated until the late 1960s and was one of the last on the line. For a time, Snow Road Station could boast of being the largest shipper of maple syrup in Canada. The station also witnessed shipments of sawlogs, pulpwood, and even foxes and eels. Although the store survives as a house, the station was disassembled and reconstructed as a cottage on nearby Millar Lake. The mill site is overgrown and leaves no trace that this was once one of the line's busiest locations.

North of Snow Road you can hop into the engineer's cab and for thirty kilometres follow the roadbed of the K&P. You can guide your train beside the marshes and lakes and through the little towns and villages, some of them now ghost towns, and recreate views that were once the sole domain of the K&P train engineers. Among all of Ontario's ghost railways there is no experience like it.

From the intersection in Snow Road drive north for about three kilometres and watch for the "K&P Trail" signs. This is not a maintained road, although during dry weather it poses no problems for most cars. Keep in mind, though, that it can become a victim of windfalls, washouts, and high spring water. It is also the width of the old

Cottagers, young and old, could travel by train from Kingston to their summer retreats around Mississippi Station. Today they must drive. (IH)

line, so when two cars approach, one must back up.

For the first five kilometres the line follows the course of Antoine Creek, leaving behind the lurching hills that characterized the line between Snow Road and Sharbot Lake. Then a clearing with a trio of old houses suddenly appears, the only remains of the one-time iron mining town of Wilbur. After operating for just a few years around the turn of the century, the mine closed, taking with it most of the mine buildings and leaving only the trio of houses and an overgrown talus heap.

Three kilometres later you emerge from the bush at Lavant Station, another once busy station location. Several houses, a hotel, and stores surrounded the small wooden station, an agglomeration that, because of the nearby Wilbur mine, was once nicknamed "Iron City." While you will no longer find any of these buildings, Lavant is still an active residential community with a number of newer homes amongst the older, railway-era houses.

For about two kilometres north of Lavant, still on the K&P Trail, you pass through the extensive marshlands that surround Graham Lake, a naturalist's paradise. Two kilometres beyond that you enter a clearing where the Folger station and sawmill were. Named for one of the K&P's early promoters, the community never developed into anything more than a rural settlement, and today still houses only a couple of families.

For five kilometres the roadbed then follows the banks of the Clyde River, here a shallow and swampy stream, to the mill town of Clyde Forks. The village itself sits about one kilometre from the line, from which a branch line forked off to the mills.

The station was only a converted boxcar, and the agent, an elderly lady who lived in the village, was often carried down to the depot in a wheelbarrow to meet arriving trains. While the mills, the station, and the branch have all vanished, many of the mill workers' modest cabins survive. Clyde Forks today has a split personality: part retirement community and part summer community, relatively isolated, and on occasion suspicious of "outsiders."

After crossing the bridge over the Clyde, you skirt Widow Lake, and enter Flower Station. Another place named for the railway builders, Flower Station was a popular destination for hunters and cottagers who travelled by train. Boxcars bearing the carcasses of a hundred deer were a frequent sight in those days. While the area remains a popular summer resort, few of Flower Station's early stores and houses have survived.

North of here you enter the most scenic portion of the route. As the trains lurched northward passengers would strain to look up at Clyde Lake Mountain on the east side of the line (about the three-kilometre mark), or enjoy the views of Clyde Lake from the other side of the train. As your "train" leaves the shore of Clyde Lake, it passes beneath Mile Lake Mountain and then skirts the shores of Mile Lake itself.

Three kilometres later, the views of Calabogie Lake begin to appear. For a little over two kilometres the line laps the shore of the lake, the peaks of the Mount St. Patrick mountains looming above its western shores. At Barryvale, the shipping point for a small farming community, the K&P Trail ends. You can continue a short distance out onto the kilometre-long causeway that crosses the lake, although it cannot be driven entirely. To resume your tour, you must drive east from Barryvale to Highway 511 and then north to Calaboogie. Look on the east side of the road for the small relocated Barryvale station as you do.

Easily one of eastern Ontario's most scenic spots, Calabogie sits on the shores of the lake whose name it shares. Original a lumber town and the site of log drives down the Madawska River, it has settled into an existence as a resort community for summer cottagers and winter skiers; the popular Calabogie Peaks lie to the west. Aside from the two sets of bridge abutments over the river, Calabogie has lost its railway heritage, and nothing remains of the days of the rail.

Sadly, that description also characterizes the remainder of the K&P. For the next 15-20 kilometres the line passes through a young forest and is difficult to follow unless you are a snowmobiler. It re-emerges only at a small hamlet known as Ashdad, before plunging once more into the woods. You can find the line at Ferguslea, located just off Highway 132 on the pioneer colonization route known as the "Opeongo Road."

Most traces of its existence in Renfrew have also vanished. Here it crossed the famous Booth Line Railway before connecting with the still active CPR. But both of Renfrew's attractive old railway stations have been lost in recent years, the stone CPR station demolished despite the residents' protests, and the smaller towered CNR station, a relic of Booth's days, removed within the last ten years.

Despite the disappointing vestiges of the line's legacy along its more northerly stretches, the K&P Trail and the central portion more than compensate.

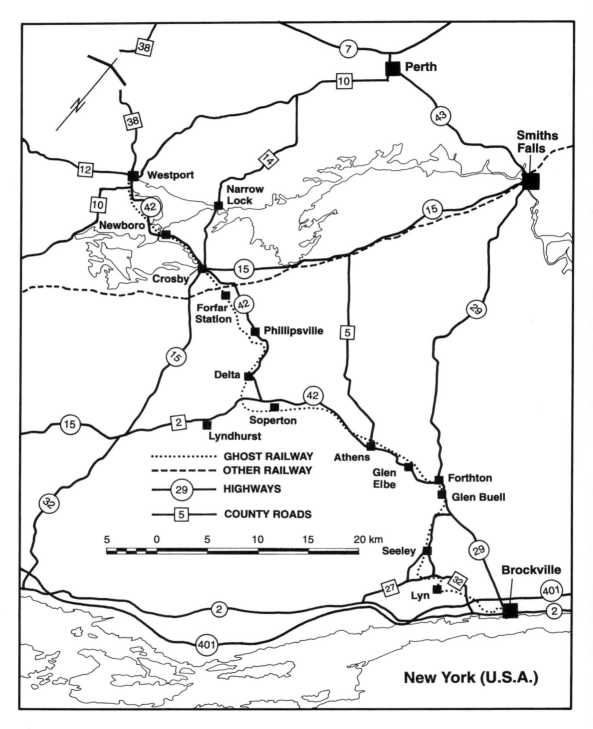

CHAPTER TWENTY

The Brockville and Westport: A Dream Cut Short

Backgrounder

The evolution of its name says it all. At first it was the "Brockville Sault Ste. Marie and North Western," then the "Brockville Westport and Sault Ste. Marie," only to finally be called the "Brockville and Westport."

As John Rudolphus Booth would succeed in doing two decades later, the promoters of the B&W wanted a rapid grain route from the west to the Atlantic. A Lake Superior terminus at Sault Ste. Marie and a rail line to the St. Lawrence port of Brockville would be just that. However, by the time the line had reached Westport the grand scheme was scrapped and the little line became no more than a local feeder to the Grand Trunk.

Chartered in 1884, the B&W route took it 60 kilometres from Brockville northwest to Westport on Big Rideau Lake. Farm produce, which included butter, cheese, feed, and fertilizer, was its major source of revenue. Sunday excursions to Westport and Newboro from Brockville were also popular. But with road improvements in the 1950s, cars and trucks proved much faster than the B&W's lurching trains, and in

1953 the line was abandoned. Despite a proposal by the Ontario Ministry of Natural Resources to create a recreational trail from Lyn Junction to Westport, the line has become indiscernible and largely forgotten.

While this excursion will reveal a few railway vestiges, it will take you through some of Ontario's oldest villages, villages that were around even before railways were known, and show you some of the province's more unusual historical treats.

All Aboard

Your route starts in Brockville, where the most interesting railway relic has nothing to do with the B&W. On Water Street, literally below the city hall, Canada's oldest railway tunnel was blasted through the stubborn grey bedrock. Excavated by the Brockville and Ottawa Railway in 1860, it is preserved in a small park, its massive oak gates bolted shut to prevent trespassing. Among Brockville's other historic structures are the city hall, a military blockhouse, a renovated main street, and the Grand Trunk station. Refurbished by Via, this

1850s station near the corner of Perth Street and Brook Road still serves passengers and is the junction between VIA's Ottawa and Montreal services.

Continue by taking Highway 2 west from Brockville for three kilometres to County Road 32 and follow it north to Lyn. The large number of newer homes in this area tells you that Lyn is rapidly becoming a dormitory town for Brockville. There was little here 125 years ago when the railway builders sought a passage through the hard wall of granite that forms a long ridge south of the village. Lyn Creek provided the perfect passage, a waterway that the railway followed northward as far as the next stop, Seeley. The right of way can be seen a

couple of blocks west of the bridge while the station was converted to a house.

From the main intersection on the east side of the creek, turn north onto County Road 32. A little more than two kilometres brings you to "Seeley Road." It's hard to believe as you look at the overgrown little gully that a village once flourished here. The right of way is barely visible on the west side of the creek, the former side-streets, houses, and stores now just an overgrown meadow.

County Road 32 continues on Highway 29. Three kilometres further on, where Highways 42 and 29 divide, sits Forthton. This tiny railway hamlet consists of a few rail-age houses and, behind the barn (at the

A mural in Athens depicts train time on the B&W.

time of writing), the little railway station. Still sporting its CNR "boxcar red" paint, now fading, and a hand-painted name "board" it sits neglected, its future anything but secure.

From Forthton follow Highway 42 west to Athens. After 2.5 kilometres you pass through the tiny community of Glen Elbe, another stop on the B&W, but nothing remains of the right of way.

Although the original station, water tower, and all other vestiges of the B&W have long since vanished, Athens has found an unusual way of celebrating its railway heritage. Among its widely known gallery of building murals is a depiction of citizens gathered at the station to watch the arrival of a steam locomotive. Painted by Lorrie Maruscak, the mural is the first one you see and it decorates the side of a former grocery store. At the town hall, obtain a guide to the other murals, and after you have viewed them, continue west on Highway 42 for eleven kilometres to Soperton, at the corner of South Lake Road.

You might miss it, however, for none of its historic crossroads buildings survives, and early timetables did not list a station at this point. Two kilometres west of the Soperton crossroads, look for County Road 2 branching west to Lyndhurst. Two kilometres more leads to the site of Lyndhurst Station. Although nothing remains, another five kilometres takes you into historic Lyndhurst,

The Delta mill, built in 1812, was one of the favourite subjects of the renowned Kingston landscape artist James Lorimer Kiersted.

the proud posessor of Ontario's oldest bridge. Built in 1857, the stone arch structure spans the tranquil waters of Lyndhurst Creek.

Return now to Highway 42 and follow it north to Delta and another historic treasure. An early mill town originally called Stevenson, Delta could claim a number of mills before the railway arrive; only one has survived. It is a stone structure and has been the subject of many paintings, one of the most famous by Kingston painter James Keirstead. The station grounds were at the west end of Main Street, a site now dominated by local fair grounds.

The next stop is Phillipsville. The string of buildings that mark Phillipsville today, along Highway 42, are a far cry from the old houses and stores that grew up around the mills on the small creek to the west. They are also some way from the station, which was located 1.5 kilometres west on County Road 2 and two kilometres north of "downtown" Phillipsville.

About three kilometres north of County Road 2 the highway makes a sharp bend to the west. The community at this bend goes by the name of Forfar and represents the site where the B&W crossed the ill-fated Canadian Northern line from Toronto to Ottawa. The site lies at end of a dirt road that leads south approximately 1.5 kilometres from the bend in the highway; however, it is now little more than a trackless overgrown meadow. The more abandoned CNR line is still clear, as is the rubble from the station that stood until the 1980s.

Highway 42 continues to Highway 15 and a community called Crosby. Despite the devastation to railway heritage that such highway intersections typically cause, you can still see a number of the old hamlet buildings that date from the railway days. The right of way crosses Highway 15 a short distance south of the intersection.

But for history enthusiasts the best on this route comes last. Five more kilometres on Highway 42 takes you to Newboro, one of the most interesting settlements on this route. While the railway and its vestiges are no longer around (the station lay at the east end of the village), take time to explore the back streets. Born at the time of the Rideau Canal, Newboro contains several buildings that date from the 1830s. Indeed Main Street, which parallels the canal, contains several former stores and hotels that pre-date the railway. And don't forget the blockhouse. It was one of a series of military buildings designed to protect the strategic canal against a possible raid from the Americans.

Many of the locks along the canal are still operated by hand, a strategy of Parks Canada designed to preserve not just the buildings along the canal, but the historic operating techniques as well. At Narrows Lock, located north of Crosby, you can see a swing bridge that is still operated in this way.

Both the highway and the railway end in Westport. A sawmill town as early as 1817, the little port boomed with the completion of the Rideau Canal in 1832. By the time the railway arrived a half century later it was already an important community. Happily, the station still stands on its original site, repainted in yellow. Located on what is now the property of the Westport Station Motel, it has served as the local Chamber of Commerce. It is simpler than the grand station originally planned.

Westport is a place to pause and spend time. Throughout its commerical and residential areas, its built heritage remains largely intact. Among the historic structures is a government fish hatchery. You can enjoy parks, either on the shores of Upper Rideau Lake or on the summit of Foley Mountain, a granite ridge that runs along the lake's north shore. From it, sweeping vistas encompass the lakes, the fields, and the village itself.

But with summer traffic from the motor boats and cars, it's dificult to picture the more pastoral era when a distant plume of smoke across the fields marked the arrival of another steam engine on the old Brockville and Westport Railway.

The original plans for the Westport station were as grand as those for the line itself. (PA)

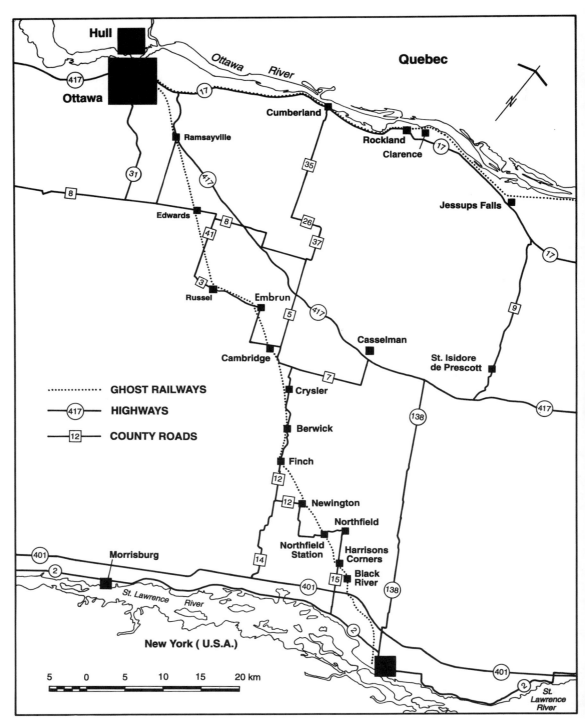

Hull

Ottawa River

Quebec

417

Ottawa

17

Cumberland

Rockland

Clarence

17

Ramsayville

31

417

35

Jessups Falls

8

Edwards

8

26

41

37

17

3

Russel

Embrun

5

417

9

Cambridge

Casselman

St. Isidore
de Prescott

7

········· GHOST RAILWAYS

Crysler

417

417 HIGHWAYS

Berwick

12 COUNTY ROADS

Finch

12

138

12

Newington

12

Northfield

401

Morrisburg

14

Northfield
Station

Harrisons
Corners

2

St. Lawrence River

15

Black
River

401

138

2

New York (U.S.A.)

5   0   5   10   15   20 km

401

2

St.
Lawrence
River

CHAPTER TWENTY-ONE

The New York and Ottawa: A Yankee Intruder

Backgrounder

In 1897 the Yanks invaded eastern Ontario. But the invasion was neither by the Fenians, nor by a leftover war party from the 1812 conflict; it was by the railway.

Anxious to link Canada's capital city with the network of railway lines that criss-crossed New York State, the promoters of the New York and Ottawa Railway (NYO), Joseph Kerr and Darby Bergin, bridged the St. Lawrence River at Cornwall, and forged their rails across eastern Ontario's rich farmlands to Ottawa. Most of the line was in the U.S., the terminus being Tupper Lake. However, the portion that crossed Ontario created a link among the communities it touched, providing service for passengers and farm products alike. Shortly after it opened, it became part of the burgeoning New York Central Railway system.

Stations were located at Black River, Harrison's, Northfield, Newington, Finch (the crossing with the CPR), Berwick, Crysler, St. Albert, Embrun, Russell, Edwards, Ramsay, Hawthorne, and, finally, Ottawa. At its peak, train service included two freights and four passenger trains a day.

During the Ottawa Exhibition, extra trains were added.

That peak did not last long, however. By 1951 passenger revenue had plunged from a high of $2000 a month 20 years earlier to less than $500 a month. In 1954 passenger service ended completely; three years later the entire railway followed.

Many of the villages through which the line passed had existed for nearly a century before, and the railway did little to change their appearance. After the death of the line a proposal to create a recreation path was scrapped. As as a result, the vestiges that were created and then left behind by the line are scant. But they do exist, and provide the back-road railway enthusiast a cross section of the often forgotten farm country of eastern Ontario.

All Aboard

Your route starts on the bike paths of Cornwall. Here is the only vantage from which to see the remains of the famous Roosevelt Bridge. Follow the trail from the centre of town to the back of the Domtar plant. There, in the St. Lawrence River, you may still see the remains of the stone supports. Three miles long, it incorporated two stationary bridges and a swing bridge. In 1934, when the bridge was planked in to allow cars to cross it as well, it was renamed the Roosevelt International Bridge. With the building of the St. Lawrence Seaway in the late 1950s, the bridge was replaced with today's high level bridge and dismantled.

While you will find plenty of railway tracks around Cornwall, none belongs to the New York Central. Most are those of the CNR and are the many sidings that serve Cornwall's massive industries. The NYO station, a long wooden building, stood east of Hoople Street at the end of Leonard Avenue, north of Second Street. Nearby you will find the Woods House Museum. The museum's counterpart, Inverarden, in the east end of town, contains photos and news stories of the railway. You'll need them, for the yards and the station have long since disappeared, with only a weedy field in their place. To satisfy railway enthusiasts, however, a Cornwall Transit Diesel can be seen in the vicinity of Woods House Museum.

The NYO's Cornwall Station was the largest on the line. (UCM)

To make your way north from Cornwall, and trace the NYO, follow Highway 2 west to Avonmore Road (County Road 15), and drive north. You will soon reach Black River Road, the route to the next of the station stops. A kilometre and a half brings you to the site of the station grounds. At a bend in the road you can see the right of way as a cindered trail. Sprawling new housing has replaced earlier historical buildings that once clustered around the station.

Return to County Road 15 and continue north. You will see the right of way cross the road at the speed limit sign for Harrison's Corners. One half kilometre west of the corner was the station ground,

although early timetables do not indicate a stop there. North from this point the OFCS snowmobile trail takes to the "rails" and provides you an opportunity to follow the line directly.

To continue by car, go north on County Road 15 from Harrison's Corners. Look for Cornwall Township Concession 9 and the Four Corners Store. This tells you that you have reached Northfield. Less than three kilometres west brings you to Northfield Station, a collection of railway-age houses, and the only place on the route to owe its origins to the railway line. It is also the only location to have retained its railway vestiges intact. You will even see the former station, now a garage, on the west side of the

The former Berwick station sits by a recreation path that follows the NYO right of way from Embrun to Russell.

road. The small green building, lacking even the traditional "bay window" of the agent, was typical of the smaller flag stations the New York Central used to replace the NYO structures along the route. A side street leads to the rest of the village where the siding and sawmill were the railway's main sources of revenue. The snowmobile trail ends here.

Turn west from Northfield Station onto Dixon Road, the first road south of the side street. Follow it four kilometres to a T intersection at County Road 12 and drive north to Newington. To enter the village turn right at the village fire hall. Newington is one of those hidden heritage treasures. Not yet ravaged by residential sprawl, or by large parking lots, Newington's old houses, churches, and stores still crowd a compact network of village streets. Older than the railway, Newington began as a stopping place on the road inland from Dickinson's Landing on the St. Lawrence River. By 1880 its population had reached 400. The railway, which skirted the east end of the village, had little impact on the townscape.

The station stood at the end of Mill Street. Nearby you will see the historic general store, Pat's, now closed, on the west side of the street, and the former station hotel, now a house, on the east side. But the station, sidings, and all vestiges of the railway have vanished entirely.

The CPR's station at Finch, gone since the 1960s, was in a style common in this section of Ontario, and served passengers of the NYO as well.

Return to County Road 12 and follow it north to Finch. Here the NYO crossed the Ontario and Quebec Railway, a line that had been absorbed into the CPR's massive network by the time the NYO crossed it. The crossing was east of Nelson Street in the east end of town. If you follow the CPR tracks east for 30 metres you will see the cement foundations of the lrailway crossing tower. A two-storey structure, the station repeated a pattern that the CPR used frequently between Smiths Falls and Vaudreuil Junction in Quebec. Ellis Hall Antiques occupies one of the main street's more historic stores and is flanked by several other interesting buildings, including a former bank building, and a former brick railway hotel.

The next stop north of Finch was Berwick where, on Union Street, you will find only a renovated feed mill to tell you that the railway passed here. The historical atlas of 1877 described the place as a "has been," and even today Berwick has little historic prosperity to show. The station, however, has survived and stands today in Embrun.

Stay on County Road 12 and drive north to Crysler. As the tall silvery steeple of the church in this French Canadian village comes into view, look for Concession Road 8/9. On the west side of County Road 12, at this point, behind a small

The CNo's former Cumberland station east of Ottawa is the only survivor on that section of line.

house with a red roof is the former Crysler railway station.

The 1877 atlas contrasted Crysler with Berwick, describing Crysler as a "new, enterprising, and thriving place of 300," where the Nation River offered water power for a grist and sawmill. Across the bridge, one kilometre down a road to the left takes you to the Home Hardware store, the site of the former station grounds. Opposite the store you can see the abutments of the the the bridge that carried the railway across the river. While in town, you can gaze at St. Rosaire Roman Catholic church, or stroll in the park that lines the south bank of the river.

Follow County Road 5 north from Crysler to a road called Route 500, drive west to rue St. Edouard, and turn south. Where the pavement ends, the right of way crossed. The route has been fenced and now grows grass for cattle. A former store with a date stone that reads 1920, and a couple of vacant lots, provide the only evidence that anything besides farms belonged here.

Follow route 500 west to St. Joseph Street and turn north to drive to Embrun. Embrun began life as a French Canadian farm village on the banks of the Castor River. By the time the railway arrived it was a bustling town. As a dormitory community for Ottawa it is experiencing a new building boom. While few of its buildings have any heritage value, you can easily find railway relics. Drive to the west end of the main street and you will find a green and grey station with a name board that reads "Embrun." Although the original Embrun station burned down shortly after the line was abandoned, authorites purchased the abandoned station building in Berwick and

moved it to its present site. It is now the starting point of a bicycle path that follows the right of way west to Russell.

The former stations from both Russell and St. Albert are now houses in Embrun. To continue to Russell follow the main street west. Or simply walk along the shady right of way. The distance is about seven kilometres.

The final station stop for this trip is Edwards. To reach this small hamlet continue west from Russell to County Road 41, take it north to Regional Road 9, and drive west less than two kilometres. Here, the right of way is overgrown and unused. Although a suburb of Ottawa, Edwards retains its former station hotel a short distance south of the road at the site of the station grounds.

Between Edwards an Ottawa there were two other stations, Ramsayville and Hawthorne. But with the boom in growth around Ottawa, the vestiges of the rail line along this section have been nearly obliterated.

In Ottawa, the NYO yards were located near the intersection of King Edward Street and Mann Avenue. For a number of years the trains of this forgotten line used the Ottawa Union Station, now a conference centre opposite the Chateau Laurier, but in later years, the railway opted for a station in its freight offices nearer its own yards. Sadly, there remain no signs of these former functions. An arena, a municipal services yard, and roads have replaced them. No period buildings, no street names, nothing survives of the New York Central in Ottawa.

Ottawa contains considerable "railroadiana" for the train enthusiast. You can visit the Museum of Science and Technology to see preserved steam locomotives, see Ottawa's former downtown station, or board the Gatineau steam train in Hull for an excursion to the picturesque mountain village of Wakefield in Quebec.

More than any other city of its size, Ottawa abounds in abandoned railway lines. Most, however, have been redeveloped as roads or trails, and have left few ghostly relics. The original GT line to the former Union Station is now a busy road, and the railway bridge that it built over the Ottawa River now carries only cars. The CPR line which led west along Scott Street from the Broad Street station has been replaced by an exclusive bus way and, west of that, a bicycle path. The city's main expressway, the Queensway, was also constructed along an abandoned right of way.

Ottawa's first station, that of the Bytown and Prescott, stood near the corner of Sus-

sex and Gruyere Streets, a location where tracks lasted until the mid 1960s. The CPR's main station was the stone chateauesque depot on Broad Street. However, after 1920, those trains began using the Grand Trunk's new station across from the Chateau Laurier, and the CPR demolished its station.

East of Ottawa, Highway 17 gives drivers a chance to follow the Canadian Northern's scenic riverside right of way from Orleans to Rockland. You can see relics of this short-lived route at Cumberland, where the former station still exists as a house (it is the second house west of the traffic lights on the south side of the highway), at Clarence where Wilson Road leads to the shore of the Ottawa River and a cottage lane which follows the roadbed, and at the South Nation River where the row of concrete bridge abutments is still evident.

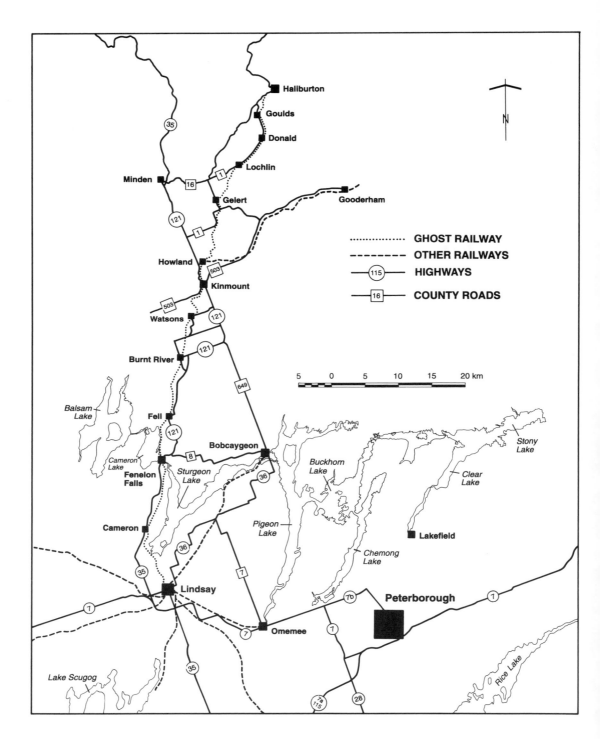

GHOST RAILWAY ....

OTHER RAILWAYS - - - - - - -

HIGHWAYS ──(115)──

COUNTY ROADS ──[16]──

The Victoria Railway: Into the Haliburton Highlands

Backgrounder

Lindsay is a busy and attractive town in the heart of Kawartha country. It's hard to believe as you drive its wide shady streets that it was once the busiest railway town in central Ontario. Today there isn't a track to be seen.

That wasn't the case when the Port Hope and Lindsay Railway (later known as the famous "Midland" Railway) rolled into town in 1857 to give the place its first railway. Within just three decades, four railways had converged on Lindsay, making it a hub of steel spokes that extended to Haliburton and Bobcaygeon to the north, to Beaverton and Midland to the west, to Peterborough in the east, and to Port Hope, Whitby, and Oshawa in the south.

All Aboard

At various times railway stations were found at King and Caroline Streets (the Port Hope and Lindsay); at Victoria and Melbourne (the Union Station between the Victoria Railway and the Whitby Port Perry and Lindsay railway); the Grand Trunk, later the CNR station, on Durham Street; and the CPR station on Lindsay Street North near Colborne.

Although all lines are now lifted and all stations removed — even though the GT and CPR stations lasted until the 1960s — you can still find evidence of Lindsay's railway legacy. The site of the CPR station is now a vacant lot, to its north the CPR bridge over Colborne, to its south a feed mill along the right of way beside Queen Street. The station itself was built with a conical witch's hat roof over the waiting room. It served for a time as a museum before demolition in the late 1960s.

The route that followed Durham Street was lifted in the early 1990s, leaving fresh evidence in the form of rotting ties and cinders in the once busy yard. The station platform can still be seen on Durham Street, although as redevelopment proposals roll in, this landscape will soon change.

The only active attempt to preserve the town's railway heritage is part of a freight train that sits on a few metres of track in the middle of Victoria Street, not far from the site of the former Union Station. The two boxcars that date from the early 1940s, the wooden caboose with the traditional CNR logo, and the yard diesel engine number 7160 appear poised to depart for Haliburton, except that beyond the display the tracks are gone, and the right of way landscaped over.

Known originally as the "Victoria Railway," the line generally parallels Highways 35 and County Road 121 between Lindsay and the town of Haliburton. It is also a route where the railway legacy has been preserved in many ways; a number of stations still stand and the route itself is a snowmobile trail for much of its length. And here and there ghost towns and ruins of industries that boomed and died with the railway stand as a more silent testimony to the days of rail. Old timetables show that trains once called at fifteen stations along the route. However, ten were mere flag stations and had no agent and few facilities.

About twelve kilometres north of Lindsay the trains puffed through Cameron. The roadbed lies about 500 metres east of Highway 35 on Long Branch Road. Used now by a snowmobile club, the right of way passes a pair of old houses that date from the days of rail, but all evidence of the two-storey sta-

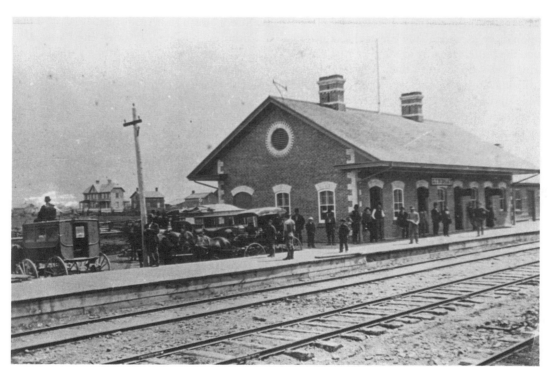

22-1 ~ One of Lindsay's four early stations.

tion that housed the section foreman, the cattle yards, and the siding have all vanished.

Railway history comes to life again in Fenelon Falls, where on the right of way at the south end of the village, Highway 35 leads you right to the old railway station. The first station, with its board and batten woodwork and arched windows, was enlarged to add a bay window and a freight shed. Now a tourist information office and art gallery, the building has been largely restored, outside and in, to its original condition.

To continue along the route follow County Road 121 north from Fenelon Falls. After seven kilometres the highway bends sharply to the east and passes a propane depot. Just behind stood another kind of depot: that of the railway at Fells. There was never a large settlement at this location, and today the name lingers on only on a few maps. The two-storey "station" doubled as a house for the section foreman and his family, with a waiting room on the ground level.

Burnt River, the next station stop, did develop into a bustling community. To reach the village turn left from the county road about nine kilometres past "Fells" and follow the green arrow. A mix of new and old buildings, the village retains the former general store, the United Church, and the Loyal Orange Lodge, another vanishing breed of building. A few metres north of this group of buildings the railway roadbed crosses the street, with the vacant station grounds on the east side. But other than the railway-era buildings and the right of way itself (now a snowmobile trail), Burnt River's railway heritage has gone.

Return to County Road 121 and continue north to Kinmount, which began as a

mill town around the falls on the Burnt River. The arrival of the railway encouraged more industries to arrive and existing industries to enlarge. With four sawmills, a grist mill, and shingle mills, Kinmount needed six sidings. But the forest was razed, leaving a solitary sawmill and a town dependent on tourism. The rails were removed in 1983.

One of the features that attracts tourists is the preserved station. Now a senior's facility, the building has been repainted in its Grand Trunk colours of yellow and red; with its front and end gables, it represents the Grand Trunk's most common small town station plan. The railway at Kinmount played a role in averting early disasters. In 1890, when a fire broke out and threatened to destroy the town, the station agent alerted the Lindsay Fire Department which arrived in less than an hour on the train. As a result most of the town was saved. Then, in 1928, as swirling flood waters closed in on them, the guests at the hotel were rowed to safety at the railway station.

To continue, take County Road 121 north from Kinmount. After one kilometre look on the east for Howland Junction Road. This side road ends a short distance away at what was once the railway's busy junction with Irondale Bancroft and Ottawa railway. The small station which replaced the original in 1917, still survives much in its railway condition near the right of way, while a short distance north lies the pit that once held a turntable for the IBO locomotives.

A short distance further north on County Road 121, look for Haliburton Road 1 and turn east. This scenic and little-used back road leads you to the partial ghost town of Gelert. Known originally as Minden Station, the place lived and died with the railway. Station Street still leads to the one time station grounds, past a vacant general store and a few old homes. The station, now long gone, was one of the largest on the line. Seventy-seven feet long and twenty-two wide, it contained a freight shed and waiting room, as well as agent's quarters with two bedrooms, a living room, and a kitchen. The right of way is now a road that you can follow on foot or by car.

North of Gelert (which is only a fraction of its original size) Haliburton Road 1 bends east to follow the right of way. It leads you to a small but intriguing relic of the past, the hamlet of Lochlin. The aging general store and a pair of other village buildings face across the road to the empty rail line.

Another three kilometres takes you to Donald and its ghostly ruins. A strange sight in the then "northern woods," Donald was home to a large factory complex that was erected by the Standard Chemical Company in 1900. The company manufactured charcoal, acetate of lime, and wood alcohol. In addition to the massive cement buildings, the company added a row of company houses that lined the track.

In 1946 Standard shut down its operations and Donald fell silent. Although the company houses no longer stand by the track, Donald Road leads you a short distance past what remains of the village to

These gaunt skeletons of the Standard Chemical Company
serve as reminders of Donald's bygone industrial days.

the massive concrete skeletons of the former industry. Although they are on private land, they can be viewed and photographed easily from the road.

The terminus of the Victoria Railway was in Haliburton, and here the story of the historic line lives like it does nowhere else. Passenger service ended along the line in 1962, and freight traffic a decade later. Finally, in the 1980s, the track was lifted and the legacy of the line that gave life to the area appeared about to vanish. But the town of Haliburton was not about to let that happen.

The right of way that followed the shore of the lake into the village has become an attractive park. Beside the main street the Haliburton Highlands Guild of Fine Arts has moved into the station and repainted it into the Grand Trunk's traditional colours of yellow and red. The track was left in place and a boxcar and caboose serve as permanent reminders of the railway era.

You can leave your car in the parking lot to explore the park and gallery, browse the downtown, or read the plaque to commemorate the rise and fall of the Victoria Railway.

The original Haliburton station was a popular spot for hunters to display their trophies. (OA)

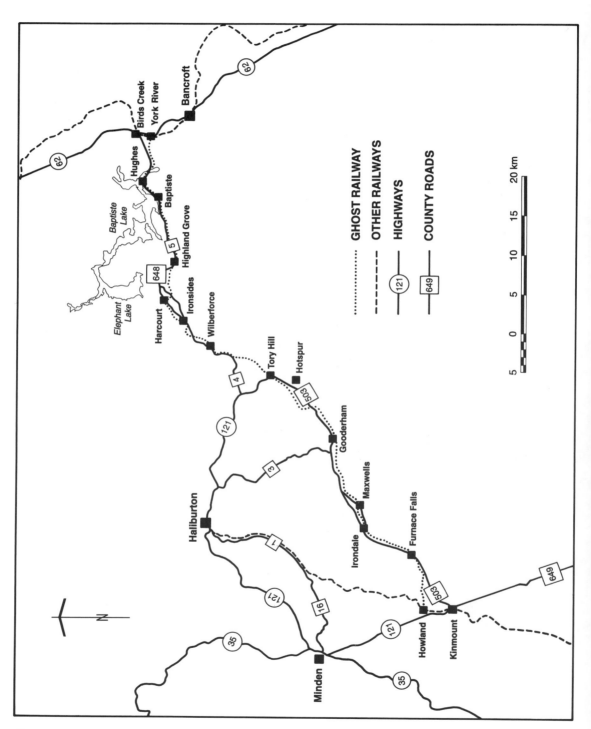

GHOST RAILWAY
OTHER RAILWAYS
HIGHWAYS 121
COUNTY ROADS 649

Bancroft
Birds Creek
York River
Hughes
Baptiste
Baptiste Lake
Highland Grove
Elephant Lake
Harcourt
Ironsides
Wilberforce
Tory Hill
Hotspur
Gooderham
Maxwells
Furnace Falls
Haliburton
Irondale
Howland
Kinmount
Minden

N

20 km
15
10
5
0
5

CHAPTER TWENTY-THREE

Highland Rails: The Irondale Bancroft and Ottawa Railway

Backgrounder

Abandoned in 1960, the Irondale Bancroft and Ottawa (IBO), a former mining railway, twisted between the lakes from Howland Junction, north of Kinmount, to Birds Creek, north of Bancroft. Although three decades of forest and field growth have obliterated much of the right of way, and redevelopment has covered most of the old station grounds, the explorer will be able to drive many of the more scenic lake side portions of the IBO roadbed, and visit some of the Haliburton Highlands' historic and rugged old mill towns that were spawned by the route.

The railway was launched around 1880 by a mining developer named W.S. Myles. From Howland Junction on the Victoria Railway (a location that he had egotistically named Myles Junction), he constructed a 6.5 mile line eastward toward his mines. That he constructed his tracks of wood rather than steel doomed his line to a short life, and within six months it was bankrupt.

A few years later Charles Pusey and Henry Howland, two more far-sighted mining men, bought Myles' failed line and by 1887 had rebuilt it to their own mining

prospect at Irondale. Here they laid out a townsite and constructed an attractive frame church. Soon the line was finished to a point four miles north of Bancroft where it met the rails of the Central Ontario Railway.

Although the mines at Irondale failed miserably, forestry fed the railway and created a string of sawmill towns along its route. But by 1900 much of the timber was also gone and the line began to lose money again. In 1909 those two ambitious builders of the Canadian Northern Railway, William MacKenzie and Donald Mann, who had earlier absorbed the Central Ontario Railway from Picton to Maynooth, added the IBO to their network. Following the bankruptcy of the CNo in 1923, the CNR became the owner. As CNR has done with most of its branch and short lines, in 1960 the government railway abandoned the IBO as well. The rails were lifted soon after and sold to make razor blades.

All Aboard

Your route begins in Kinmount, a highland mill town that is also on the Victoria Railway (see Chapter 22), and follows the IBO eastward through a land of lakes and rocky cliffs, past towns which thrive and others which died, to its junction with the COR. From Howland eastward the line closely followed the shore of the Irondale River and now crosses County Road 503 about one kilometre west of the Irondale River bridge. From the small riverside picnic park beside the bridge you can make out the railway embankment on the far bank.

The line continues along the south bank of the river to the ghost town of Irondale about nine kilometres further along. To reach the site turn south at the Irondale Road and drive one kilometre to a T intersection. Turn right and drive a short distance to see the old Pusey church, still standing, and the site of the vanished village of Irondale.. Besides the church Irondale contained three hotels and a number of simple log homes, one of which stood until the late 1980s. The large wooden station burned in 1931 and was replaced with a pair of boxcars.

By continuing west along the road you will come to the river, and on the north side of the road you will see the abutments of the IBO. From Irondale to Gooderham the line followed the north bank of the river, only portions of which remain visible from the

The Irondale church is the only survivor of the days when Irondale was a raucous iron mining town, and the reason for the building of the IBO.

south side of County Road 503. Gooderham has retained much of its rustic highland atmosphere, although the landmark sawmill and the first station are both gone and the railway line is no longer evident.

The next IBO station stop east of Gooderham is Tory Hill. The village is quieter now and newer homes mingle with old. Otherwise there is little of the main street and the businesses that thrived with the railway.

West of the intersection of County Roads 503 and 121, the centre of Tory Hill, the old roadbed is still discernible between the road and McCue Lake. The last Tory Hill "station," a boxcar, stood at this corner until the late 1980s, used for storage. Take County Road 121 north for five kilometres to Haliburton Road 4, the Essonville Road, and follow the old rugged pioneer road east to Otter Lake Road and Wilberforce the road is built upon the IBO roadbed.

Wilberforce is another place that mixes old and new. While here and there railway-era buildings contrast with the newer mini-malls, the extensive sawmill yards of the Wilberforce Veneer Plant are firmly rooted in the town's origins. The Wilberforce station, another boxcar-sized structure , ignominiously lived out its dying days as a storage shed for beer empties before being razed. East from County Road 648, Schofield

This loggers' hotel at Baptiste, now a bed and breakfast, predates the arrival of the rails.

Drive follows the right of way as it skirts the veneer plant and hugs the shore of Pusey Lake. Although scenic, the public section of the road ends after a mere one kilometre at a private drive.

A few kilometres east of Wilberforce on Highway 648 the right of way reappears, this time as the Little and Upper Cardiff Lake Roads. It follows the north shore of the lake of the same name for about two kilometres, where the Zum Waldhaus Bed and Breakfast is located, before it reunites with the highway.

To the railway it was Mumford, today it is Harcourt, but strangely both names still appear on some maps. Although it was the next station stop east of Wilberforce, it re-

tains little to evoke the days of rail; few IBO-era buildings have survived, and the right of way is now a playground. By contrast, far more history has survived in Highland Grove. Among the several older buildings are two rustic old-time general stores (one of which is now closed). The station grounds at the end of a short side street leading west of the highway once held a two-storey station with a freight room and agent's quarters, and beside it extensive cattle yards. No evidence of any of this has survived, however.

Between Highland Grove and Baptiste, IBO passengers could enjoy the most scenic portion of the route. Here the rail line first hugged the shores of Jordan Lake and Dia-

The Baptiste Lake flag station was small but, in the summer, busy.

mond Lake, and then passed beneath the high cliffs that loom above the shores of Baptiste Lake. Today, the road follows that same scenic path. From Highland Grove simply follow Diamond Lake Road easterly. Jordan Lake and Diamond Lake appear after two and four kilometres respectively, while the tree- and cliff-lined waters of Baptiste Lake come into view after about seven.

At the village of Baptiste itself stands one of the single most historic structures along the line, one that predates the railway. Known today as Grants Country Inn and General Store, this three-storey wooden building began life as a loggers' hotel more than a century ago. The store which occupies the western end of the building still boasts a pressed tin ceiling, while the dining room displays photographs of trains in the Baptiste station. The right of way and station grounds which were located halfway down the hill between the hotel and the lake have both since disappeared beneath landscaping.

Between Baptiste Lake and Highway 60, the road and the railway part company. In the early years this section of the IBO remained incomplete until the COR line was pushed north from Bancroft. Today, except for a causeway through the swampy waters of the aptly named Mud Creek at the east end of Baptiste Lake, the little line disappears once more. The road continues as the South Baptiste Lake Road east to Highway 60, where the legacy of the old COR lingers on.

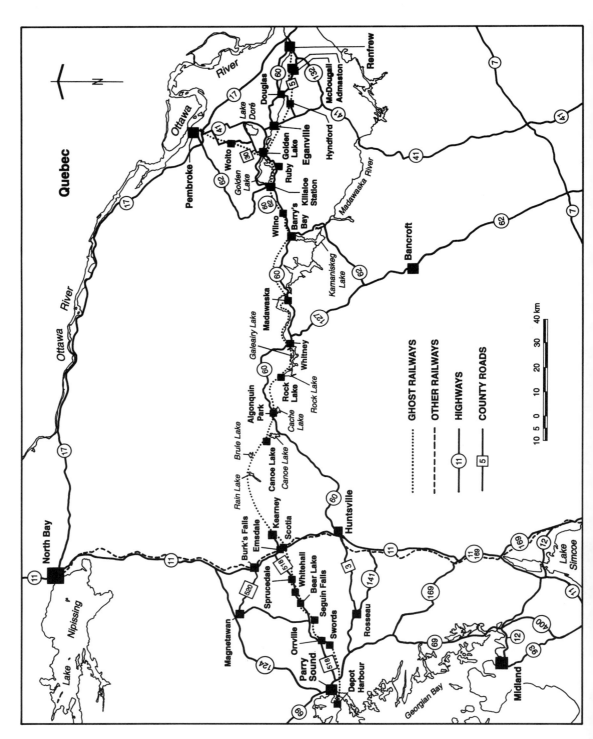

CHAPTER TWENTY-FOUR

The Ottawa Arnprior and Parry Sound: John Booth's Ghost Town Trail

Backgrounder

It was the shortest grain route to the Atlantic through the wilds of central Ontario, its trains arriving and departing every twenty minutes. It was the longest railway ever built and owned by one man in Canada. It was the Ottawa Arnprior and Parry Sound Railway, the line that John R. Booth built. Today it is a trail of ghost towns.

Despite his humble origins as a Waterloo, Quebec, farmer's son, John R. Booth was destined for greatness. Shortly after establishing his own mill in Hull, the newcomer stunned the Ottawa lumber barons by contesting the prized contract for the construction of the parliament buildings, and winning. Ever the pragmatist, he simply underbid his more established rivals by engaging unemployed longshoremen from the docks of Montreal.

With money in his pocket and with railways the only way to ship lumber, in 1872, Booth bought a pair of floundering railways which gave him the right to cross the St. Lawrence and link with the Vermont Cen-

tral Railway at the U.S. border. In 1879 his Canada Atlantic Railway was born, an empire that extended from Ottawa to the Atlantic.

His next step was to expand his timber supply. When the rich timber limits in Algonquin Park came up for auction, the wily Booth sent his cousin to inspect them and, buoyed by that report, he again outmanoeuvred his more conservative rivals. For the limits that he bought for an unheard of $40,000 he would, five years later, be offered more than a million. He refused.

He then turned his eyes toward Georgian Bay. A rail route to that water body would not only provide access to his new timber stands, but would also enable him to capture the burgeoning prairie grain trade. First he purchased the charter of the Parry Sound Colonization Railway — an effort by Parry Sounders to link their town with the Northern and Pacific Western Railway at Burk's Falls — and started building westward to meet it. His route took him northwestward into the mountains of Renfrew County along the course of the Madawaska River through Algonquin Park, and then over the divide and down into the struggling pioneer settlements of Parry Sound district.

The problem came at Parry Sound. While the charter of the Parry Sound Colonization Railway stipulated that the town be the terminus, local landowners held out for prices that Booth simply refused to pay. In any event, on an island six miles away he found a harbour that was far superior to that at Parry Sound and there he ended his railway. Beside his terminus he created the town of Depot Harbour, a bustling port that would rival established communities like Collingwood and Midland, and then become Ontario's largest ghost town.

All Aboard

The remains of this historic railway exhibit three distinct characteristics. West of Algonquin Park it is almost entirely a snowmobile trail, hikable in summer, a few sections even driveable by car. The part east of the park has largely been sold to adjacent owners. Here the right of way, even that which follows the banks of the Madawaska, is mostly off limits or built over. In the park itself, however, even though the Ministry of Natural Resources (MNR), the park's curator, has removed all

The unique style that Booth used on many of his Booth line stations is found now only in Barry's Bay.

buildings, the legacy lives on in lively and interesting annotated hiking trails.

From Renfrew to Huntsville plan on spending most of your route on Highway 60, west of Huntsville on Highway 518. From downtown Renfrew, Highway 132 leads you west past Renfrew Junction, where Booth's line crossed the old K&P. After 5.6 kilometres turn north onto winding County Road 5. The station village for McDougall, at the seven kilometre mark, lies two kilometres east in Admaston, a one-time crossroads hamlet that has lost nearly all traces of the railway.

Seven kilometres later the road turns sharply north and leads to the three buildings that survive at Douglas Station. As you enter Douglas itself, a few kilometres further, you cross the abandoned roadbed of the Atlantic and Northwestern Railway, CPR's failed attempt to beat Booth to Georgian Bay. Once a busy farming and lumbering town, Douglas still retains two of its old hotels, both on the east side of the main street. From Douglas follow County Road 22 west for about five kilometres to Hyndford, an early farm community that boomed when Booth hit town. The railway lies on the south side of the road, crossing at an angle just before the intersection.

From the intersection continue west until you come to Highway 41 and follow it north to Eganville., where at least on part of Booth's legacy lives. Here you will still find the old Eganville station, its platform, and the right of way. After serving for several years as an antique store, it fell vacant and was offered for sale. Although downtown redevelopment has obliterated all trace, Eganville was as far as the CPR's rival Georgian Bay route got. After losing a court fight to wrest from Booth the rights to build its line through Hagarty Pass, the only route through the Black Donald Mountains, the CPR called it quits and built its terminus, a small witch's hat-style station, here. It was demolished in the 1960s when the CPR stopped using the branch line. The town still contains a number of buildings from its lumber days, including an aging grist mill.

From the centre of Eganville take Highway 60 fourteen kilometres west to Golden Lake, where the little used Pembroke and Southern Railway branched off to lead northeastward to Pembroke. Although abandoned officially in 1961, it was seldom used before that. Only two small stations, at Locksley and Woito, were located on this now largely obliterated line. A look around Golden Lake village will reveal that the many workers' houses date from the days of rail, but you won't find much else. The right of way and the station, located south of the village on the south bank of the Bonnechere River, have been replaced by a road. In fact, the most interesting structure in the village had nothing to do with the Booth Line at all. South of the main intersection sits a two-storey blacksmith shop, constructed of logs, and complete with an ancient glass gas tank.

While the right of way continues south of Golden Lake, you may follow Highway 60 north of it. Although there is nothing to see of the line or its structures (the only station stop was at Ruby), the highway does present some pleasant vistas across the lake as well as picnic spots from which to enjoy them. It then bypasses Killaloe Station, and you might as well do the same, for despite the name, no vestiges of the railway are evident anywhere: station and track have long since vanished. The older parent village of Killaloe remains, however, a tiny mill town on the southern outskirts of the station settlement that outgrew it.

About twenty kilometres west of Killaloe, still on Highway 60, the tall spires of the Wilno Catholic church come into view. Wilno, which is Canada's first Polish settlement, is also the site of the "battle" of Hagarty pass. The deep gully that lies north of the highway was the only feasible route for a rail line to penetrate the formidable Black Donald Mountains. As the surveyors for both the CPR and the Booth Line raced up the pass, their bosses were locked in a court fight to determine which should have the rights to it. Not surprisingly Booth won, and the CPR surveyors went home, their hopes for a line from Ottawa to Georgian Bay stalled at Eganville.

Wilno itself remains a picturesque collection of turn-of-the-century stores and houses perched on the hillside. At their feet the line skirts a small creek. You can see a small railway bridge that crossed the creek, but of the station and other railway structures, nothing remains.

Fortunately this is not the case at Barry's Bay. A lumber town of old (it still has a sawmill) and head of steamship navigation on Lake Kaminiskeg, Barry's Bay has preserved its station, its railway water tank, and, across from the station, the traditional

The Joe Lake station was built of logs to give arriving tourists a feel of the wilderness. (APM)

railway hotel. Like station hotels all across Canada it hosted travelling salesmen, and still wets the whistle of local and visiting tavern-lovers alike.

The station style that you see in Barry's Bay was distinctive to Booth's line. With its almost top-heavy second storey and gable, the style was repeated in most of the agent depots east of the park and in at least two west of it. The Barry's Bay station is the only survivor, however, and today the town is restoring it for a new use as a community building.

Between Barry's Bay and Madawaska the Booth Line lies deep in the woods, inaccessible and only occasionally visible. As you enter Madawaska from the east, you see the long trestle and causeway over the Madawaska River.

As he laid his rail westward, Booth ignored pressure to locate his divisional point at Barry's Bay, and instead chose Madawaska inside his timber limit to construct his crew's quarters, repair facilities, and a wooden five-stall roundhouse. In 1914 the Grand Trunk, which had bought Booth out ten years earlier for $14 million, replaced Booth's smaller roundhouse with a fourteen-stall structure made of concrete.

The Booth Line hugs the shore of the Madawaska River all the way to the village of Whitney. However, when the MNR failed to acquire the right of way, it was sold to private interests and much of it is inaccessible in this section. The eastern gateway to Algonquin Parkway, Whitney is a small collection of houses, restaurants, and stores. Although it crosses the highway on the west side of the river, the right of way is scarcely

visible and all evidence that the town even had a railway link has gone. However, you can park your car here, on the shores of Galeairy Lake, and canoe beside the right of way as it skirts the north shore of this attractive lake.

This brings you to the second section of your search: the route through Algonquin Park.

Created in 1893 as a "national" park, Algonquin carries on Booth's tradition: logging. Although billed as a "wilderness," Algonquin echoes not just to the loon, but to the throaty rumble of logging trucks at less busy times of the year. However, in the park's wilderness portions, park authorities have provided a wide range of recreational opportunities: campgrounds, canoe routes, a modern museum and restaurant, and hiking trails along Booth's line. But because it has long been the MNR's policy to remove historical structures on crown land, no Booth structures survive. However, three hiking routes follow, at least in part, the old right of way. To give the hikers an historic view of what they are following, small booklets provide commentary on the long vanished railway features that once existed along the route.

And of these there were many. Within the park, Booth or other lumber companies established no fewer than four towns — Rock Lake (originally outside the park boundary but later included when the park expanded), Canoe Lake, Brule Lake, and Rain Lake while the Grand Trunk added several hotels, the most popular of which were the Hotel Algonquin, the Mowat Lodge, and the Highland Inn, perhaps the best known of all. In addition, members of Booth's family constructed their own summer retreat. Known as the Barclay Estate, it boasted landscaped gardens, tennis courts, and a spectacular vista across Rock Lake. Bridges and stations also dotted the line as it wound through Booth's timber limits.

Stations, hotels, estates, and towns — today they are all gone, but the hiking trails help you relive them. The easternmost trail of the three is appropriately called Booth's Rock Trail and you can reach it by following the directional signs a short distance west of the museum, which is close to the park's eastern gate. When you reach the Rock Lake campgrounds you have reached the Booth Line. From here to the start of

the hiking trail about two kilometres to the southeast, you are on the old roadbed. Park and hike the roadbed as it follows the shore of the lake to the peninsula where the Barclay Estate stood. Built by Judge George Barclay around 1900, it remained in use until 1953. Although it was offered to the government as a hospital, the offer was turned down and the place demolished. The adjacent gardener's house, known as Men-wah-tay, met a similar fate.

West of the Rock Lake campground you can follow the roadbed a short distance to an original Booth bridge, across which, until the 1980s, lumber trucks rumbled to and from a large sawmill. The campground itself marks the site of the tiny Rock Lake sta-

Built by Booth as his western terminus, Depot Harbour was the largest town in Ontario to become a ghost town. (OA)

tion and the settlement of a half dozen or so houses that stood nearby. No trace remains.

The next accessible portion of the railway is the Mizzy Lake Trail, west of the Booth Rock Trail. While the central portion of the Mizzy Lake Trail from Science Lake to Wolf Howl Lake follows the roadbed, there were no railway vestiges here, and the trail is more appropriately considered a wildlife trail. However, a private logging and lodge access road continues along the roadbed west from Wolf Howl Lake, past the site of the Joe Lake and Canoe Lake stations, all the way to Brule Lake.

At Joe Lake the line crosses the popular portage between Canoe Lake and Big Joe Lake. The crossing marks the site of the wooden Hotel Algonquin and the tiny log station that served it. A short distance west the Canoe Lake station, designed like the one in Barry's Bay, guarded the spur line that led to the Gilmour Company sawmill and town on the shore of the lake. Named Mowat, the town housed as many as 700 lumbermen, mill workers, and family until shortly after the turn of the century. The town boarding house became the Mowat Lodge, a summer resort that attracted a young Canadian painter named Tom Thompson. It was from here that he embarked upon his ill-fated canoe ride, a ride from which he did not return.

Although the station has long disappeared, a number of the town buildings are used as summer cottages. When the leases run out, however, they too will be demolished.

A smaller mill town stood at Brule Lake and outlasted that at Canoe Lake by a number of years. But other than an overgrown clearing, no-one would know it existed.

Near the western limit of the park, accessible only to canoers, stood yet another sawmill town, Rain Lake. It has left no trace either, although the cindered roadbed is clearly visible.

But it is the Track and Tower Trail that gives you your longest hike along Booth's line and a look at the site of the disaster that killed it. The trail starts from a parking lot 25 kilometres in from the west gate. About two kilometres from the start you come to Cache Lake, where Booth built a pair of trestles to carry his trains over the bay. In 1933 a sudden surge of ice crashed against the trestles, and unwilling to spend the half million dollars required to repair them, the depression-weary CNR simply abandoned that section of the route. From then on, trains from the east stopped at Madawaska, those from the west at the Highland Inn.

This trail also leads you to the locations of two of the largest bridges that Booth built, those over the Madawaska. They were demolished in the 1940s and today only the concrete abutments remain.

Before leaving the park, stop in the parking lot at Cache Lake. While you can hike eastward on the roadbed, to the west, now within a park maintenance yard, lies the site of the popular Algonquin Park station, the subject of many a promotional photograph, and the Highland Inn. Apart from the asphalt station platform hidden in the pine plantation, nothing remains.

One of the best ways to appreciate Booth's days is a visit to the Algonquin Park museum. This new structure houses a gift shop, a theatre, a restaurant with one of the park's best views, and a large collection of Booth era photographs. To see the photos you must make arrangements with the curators, but it's worth it, if only because so much of Booth's heritage itself has been needlessly removed from the landscape.

The third portion of your Booth Line experience lies west of the park. Most of the route, from Highway 69 near Parry Sound to Sprucedale on Highway 518, is owned by the MNR and known as the Seguin snowmobile trail. Between Sprucedale and the park, it is also a snowmobile trail, and although owned by the province, is neither managed nor maintained by it.

Thus it is a route that you can hike, ski or snowmobile, although there is little scenery to entice you for that reason alone. You can just as easily see most features by driving from railway town to railway town. The towns came with Booth, and they died with the end of rail traffic. Many are ghost

John Rudolphus Booth, lumber magnate and railway builder, was Canada's richest entrepreneur in his time. (PC)

towns, nearly all far less important than they were in their heyday. To start this section, take Highway 60 westward from the park to Highway 11 just north of Huntsville. From this intersection drive north 32 kilometres to Highway 518. Ten kilometres to the east sits Kearney.

Once a busy sawmill town and station stop on the Booth Line, this picturesque lit-

tle community is now the centre of a small tourist area. With its row of railway-era stores on a main street that looks over the Magnetawan River, as well as its many lumber era houses and historic churches, Kearney is more than worth a visit. The site of the old station and of the Booth line itself lies about one kilometre south of the stores. Other than the roadbed, there is nothing to tell you that there was ever a railway here. The station was one of those two-storey "Booth" styles that you saw at Barry's Bay.

The busiest point on Booth's line was a place called Scotia Junction. Here the line crossed the equally busy Grand Trunk line from Toronto to North Bay. Switches and sidings filled a large field, while the attractive, turreted station sat tucked into the diamond where the two routes crossed. The simpler, single-storey station that replaced it in 1914 was demolished in the 1960s. The site lies south of Emsdale on Highway 592. Near the intersection of Edgar Street and Highway 592, a small bridge crosses over the right of way, here a snowmobile trail sunk into a forested gully.

Nearby, you can see a number of old houses that date from those historic days.

But among them are a number of newer homes as well. Edgar Street leads west from the highway to a former boarding house, the only heritage structure left that has direct links to railway days. Opposite the boarding house, a large field marks the location of the yards and the station. Except for the single CNR track, today it lies empty.

If the little railway towns west of Scotia have retained much of their history, it has been due not as much to active preservation as to the thankful absence of insensitive "modernization" that would obliterate it. Stores, churches, and hotels have managed to survive simply because the demand to replace them has not yet been felt.

The best example of this is Sprucedale. Once the most important shipping point west of the park for farm produce, as well as for lumber, it is still the focal point for the rural community that surrounds it. While only a single combination hardware/general store/restaurant remains in operation, you can see several other old buildings that bear the unmistakable boom-town facade that reveals their former commercial function. Some are on the highway while others are south on Stisted Street, the main cross street in town.

The former high school is now a seniors' club, while the white-frame United church still offers Sunday sermons. The Booth Line crosses the highway at the town sign and parallels the road on the north, passing immediately behind the historic Sprucedale Hotel. One of the most historic structures in the district of Parry Sound, it is an original pioneer hotel and still offers cold liquid refreshment to the traveller in its Hunters' lounge. The station, a simpler, single-storey Grand Trunk pattern, stood west of the hotel.

You will be able to see the line to the north of the highway for about three kilometres west of Sprucedale, except in summer when vegetation blocks this view. About 5.5 kilometres west of Sprucedale look for Bourdeau Road. If you miss it you will have missed the ghost town of Whitehall. Two empty stores and an abandoned house are about all that survive of the original settlement.

You can see the right of way by driving a short distance south on Axe Lake Road. Signs on it point to Sprucedale and Bear Lake; thus Booth's abandoned railway line is better signed than the highway itself. It is one of Ontario's premier snowmobile trails and provides winter enthusiasts with a unique opportunity to probe the past. At 7.7 kilometres west of Sprucedale, the right of way crosses the highway again and follows a steep embankment. A short hike will take you north to the shore of a nearby lake and one of the few scenic portions on this section of Booth's line.

Although Bear Lake, originally known as Jarlsberg, has few buildings that date from Booth's days, St. Olaf's church more than compensates. This white-frame church with the tilting steeple sits picturesquely on a rocky knoll by the highway at the eastern end of the village. In the centre of the village you can see a log structure that forms part of a local museum display. The right of way, which stood some distance to the north, is out of sight of the highway.

The rough and twisting nature of the highway west of Bear Lake gives you an appreciation of the difficulties that confronted both the railway builders and the original pioneer settlers, but few suffered more than those who settled the colonization roads. A network of 25 government-built roads that led into the wilds of what we now call cottage country, these pioneer trails were, with their free land, touted by the government of the 1850s as panacea for the land-starved farmers of southern Ontario. In reality the scheme was a sop to lumber companies that wanted men, horses, and produce. The land was stony and unproductive, although the government hid that fact from the settlers, and when the lumber companies left, the settlers faced starvation.

One of the colonization roads was the Nipissing Road which you meet west of Bear Lake and can follow south from Highway 518 to the ghost town of Seguin Falls. Originally a colonization road "stopping place" a short distance north of the intersection, Seguin Falls moved south in 1896 when Booth railway builders appeared from the woods. At its peak it had a hotel, school, church, stores and a sawmill. Its station, however, was never more than a shack-sized flag stop. When the trains stopped coming, Seguin Falls' hopes for survival began to dwindle. A few hardy inhabitants stayed on, but the decline in lumbering and the lure of the city lights doomed the old pioneer town.

In his 1966 newspaper column, the *Toronto Telegram's* Harvey Curell described it as a "ghost town worth visiting." It sat there silent with its hotel, school, and a handful of houses, large and small but mostly vacant. Since then the hotel has burned down and seasonal tenants have moved into many of the old homes. It may not be the ghost town that it once was, but it is still worth a visit. The Seguin snowmobile trail barges right through the centre, and is one of the more heavily travelled portions of the trail.

An interesting side trip, or even a trip in its own right, lies north along the Nipissing Road. It leads you past abandoned farms, through ghost towns and into cemeteries where inscriptions describe the horrible hardships that confronted the area's inhabitants, and ends on the shores of Lake Nipissing.

About 35 kilometres from Sprucedale, Highway 518 enters Orrville. The name on the station, however, was Edgington, and that building stood on the right of way, at the end of James Street near the blue village highway marker. The lumber from the station, another "Booth" style, was used to build a house nearby. The most populated community on the route, this gathering place for local residents and cottagers contains a small pub, an attractive wood-frame United church, and a short distance south on the Star Lake Road, the old town blacksmith shop.

Four kilometres west of Orrville the Swords Road leads south to yet another ghost town. Despite newer growth in the surrounding area, Swords retains its ghostly appearance with a pair of abandoned railway-age houses, and the weathered former general store, north of which the Booth line crosses the road. During the days of rail, Swords was the site of the Maple Lake Hotel, the popular destination of canoeists anxious to try the Muskoka Lakes. One such group of regulars from the U.S. called themselves the "Buffalo Flyers."

West of Swords the roadbed disappears into the bush, and between Swords and Highway 69 it can be seen from the road in only a few places. Snowmobilers, however, can put themselves "in" the cab of the Booth Line train engineers and follow the right of way as it passes through the forests and over the swamps and creeks. Some portions are driven by car, but the route is not maintained for that use.

At the end of the Booth Line are the ghosts of Depot Harbour, the town that Booth built, and the largest town in Ontario to become a ghost town. Enter Parry Sound and take the Great North Road to Rose Point. Here you cross the railway swing bridge that still opens to allow boats to pass. The road leads through the Parry Island Indian Reservation to the one-time port of Depot Harbour.

When Booth took over the charter of the Parry Sound Colonization Railway, his intention was to put the port facilities at Parry Sound. However, the high land prices asked by local land owners, and the lure of a much superior harbour, drew Booth to Parry Island. Here he built a town he could call his own. On a dozen city blocks he constructed a two-storey school, three churches, a large hotel, and a townsite with 110 houses. There were railway offices, yards, immense grain elevators, and the railway roundhouse. By providing the western grain growers with their shortest route to the Atlantic — straight through Algonquin Park — Depot Harbour was one of the leading ports on the Great Lakes and threatened to eclipse rivals like Collingwood, Midland, and Owen Sound.

The CNR eventually acquired Booth's railway and closed the facilities in Depot Harbour in favour of those at South Parry, a short distance south. In 1933, when the Cache Lake trestle was damaged by ice, the CNR stopped through trains altogether. No longer the shortest grain route to the Atlantic, Depot Harbour lost its advantage over its rivals and became a ghost town. All buildings were removed in the early 1950s and today only foundations, weedy sidewalks, and the empty ruin of the roundhouse lurk in the silent young forest.

Despite having been unique among Canada's railways, the heritage of the Booth Line is sadly neglected. Vestiges that survive do so by accident rather than by design. The efforts in Barry's Bay and the information in the Algonquin Park museum are the exceptions. Other than that, towns and railway features lie deteriorating, their story uncelebrated. Nevertheless, this rail-lovers' route provides enough sights to ensure that it is still one of the best.

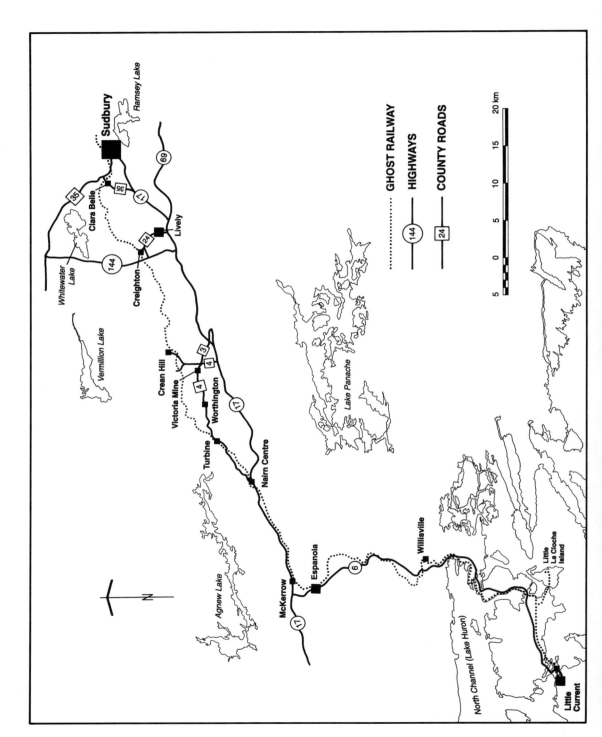

CHAPTER TWENTY-FIVE

The Algoma Eastern Railway: The Mines of Yesterday

Backgrounder

Sudbury today is a bustling city, a vibrant community that owes its prosperity to its mines. But a century ago, when a prospector discovered copper and another, unknown mineral in the woods near a quiet railway junction named Sudbury, he could have little realized that his discovery in the wilderness would eventually lead to the grown of a metropolis.

The unknown mineral was nickel. Although lacking in appeal for jewellery, nickel was vital as an industrial mineral. The copper drew the mining companies there in the first place, but the nickel certainly kept them there. Discoveries occurred everywhere and the woods west of Sudbury suddenly sprouted mine shafts and headframes. The boom was on.

Francis Clergue, discoverer of the deposits at Wawa and the builder of the Algoma Central Railway, knew a promising railway route when he saw it. To tap the mines west of Sudbury he set out to build the Algoma Eastern Railway (AER). In 1900 he took over the defunct charter of the Manitoulin and North Shore Railway (MNSR). This route was originally proposed to link Manitoulin Island and Sudbury and then establish a railway ferry service to Tobermory on the Bruce Peninsula. Although it joined the CPR in downtown Sudbury, which twenty years earlier had completed its first "main" line to Sault Ste. Marie, the AER shared its station with the Canadian Northern. Its yards were in Little Britain, a residential community west of Frood Road in northwest Sudbury.

West of town, in the forest, lay the mining frontier: Clarabelle, Creighton, Gertrude, O'Donnell, Crean, Victoria, and Worthington were all mining centres along the AER, and each had its own community of tough miners. Beyond the mines, the AER entered an area where pioneer farmers had hacked their rough bush farms from the northern forests, and where lumbermen wrenched out pine logs for mills at places like Espanola. The railway then turned abruptly south and made its way through one of Ontario's most rugged mountain ranges before escaping onto the flat limestone plains of Manitoulin Island and the terminus at Little Current.

With mines and mills in full swing, the AER was one of Ontario's most promising railways. In fact it was one of the few in Canada to escape the clutches of the new Canadian National Railway created in 1918 to take over the many lines rendered bank-rupt by World War I. However, by 1924 Clergue's charter for the MNSR had lapsed and the CPR looked longingly at his money-making railway. Now, what the CPR wants the CPR usually gets, and by 1930 the AER belonged to the CPR, "leased" for a period of 999 years. But in less than six years the CPR had got out its axe and had begun chopping back its new acquisition. By 1960 the portion between Creighton and Espanola lay abandoned.

The abandonment was no surprise, for the CPR's original "main" line paralleled the AER from Sudbury all the way to McKerrow. From that point the CPR's line continued west to Sault Ste. Marie while the AER turned south to Manitoulin; those portions the CPR retained.

All Aboard

The AER's Sudbury station, a stone-turreted station that it shared with the CNo, is gone now, a victim of urban renewal. In stood in an area known as the "Flour Mill," near Leslie Street east of rue Notre Dame. The AER then moved in with the CPR in an attractive sta-tion that still stands on Elgin Street, although it

The stone station that the AER shared with the CNo was removed in the name of urban renewal.

is used now only by passengers who board the local train to White River. AER track still exists through Sudbury, past the site of the AER yards at Little Britain (west of Frood Street, three blocks north of Elm) and the new aluminum "station" at Clarabelle, to Creighton.

But Creighton is the town that disappeared. More than a mine, Creighton was a sizeable town. Owned by INCO, the owner of the mine, at its peak it could boast 1,200 residents living in 400 houses, with churches, schools, and a vibrant shopping district. Then in 1986 the bad news came. INCO was unable to upgrade the water and sewer services to comply with the strict new provincial standards, and the town was to close down. Within a mere

two years the residents were gone, the town bulldozed into oblivion.

Follow the Trans-Canada Highway west of Sudbury to Highway 144 and turn north. After four kilometres turn east onto Regional Road 24. You soon reach the mine, which still operates. Park here and follow the cindered side streets that lead away from both sides of Regional Road 24. You can walk the sidewalks but see only the foundations and the ghosts of a community that thousands once called home. Where Regional Road 24 meets Highway 144, you can also see the end of track on the AER. Three kilometres west of Creighton, hidden now by the regenerating forests, are the abandoned ruins of the Ger-

The mining town of Creighton on the AER was bulldozed because the owner, Inco, could not afford to upgrade its in-ground services.

trude mine. However, the ruins of the O'Donnell roasting yard are harder to mask. In 1928, at a time when environmental threats were seldom appreciated, the roasting yard at O'Donnell posed such a concern that the provincial government ordered it closed. One half century later, the land remains barren.

The Crean Mine, next on the line, lasted longer and still sees activity. The residential community, however, has moved away and workers now commute to the site. Mine and bush roads follow the AER roadbed west of the Crean to the now silent site of the Victoria Mine. Although the nickel lay along the AER, the townsite, a large community now completely vanished, was five

kilometres south on the CPR line. You can reach the Crean and Victoria mine sites by following Regional Road 4 north from Regional Road 3 near Whitefish, on the Trans-Canada Highway, 15 kilometres west of Sudbury. At the Crean Hill sign turn north again. After two kilometres the road forks; Crean mine is to the right, Victoria to the left.

The ghost town of Victoria consists now of only a talus heap and, where the main street once stood, a cinder trail in a meadow.

One kilometre north of the fork in the road, a bush road again follows the right of way for six difficult kilometres to the site of the Worthington station. It is best to reach

The tracks of the AER and the CPR met at McKerrow, where this attractive station stood until 1983, when the CPR demolished it.

this location by returning to Regional Road 4 and following it west to Worthington.

Another mining ghost town, Worthington has come back to life, if only modestly. When the shafts beneath suddenly gave way in 1927 much of the town went with it. CPR trains were forced to re-route onto the AER; it was the ghost railway's busiest time. Even though the CPR was rebuilt, the town never fully recovered. You can still follow the cindered village streets through grassy meadows. The Company Store is the only business left in town. Regional Road 4 turns north here and after 2.5 kilometres you cross the abandoned right of way of the AER.

Beyond Worthington, the AER leaves mining country. Return south on Regional Road 4 to the Nairn Road and continue west. Near the junction of the road to High Falls, five kilometres west, the AER and the CPR lines draw to within a few yards of each other at a place called Turbine. So named because of a hydro plant four kilometres upstream on the Spanish River, the settlement has no buildings of any kind.

Both lines and the road continue southwest to Nairn, a community that once had two stations. A CPR townsite, the grid streets all lie south of the CPR tracks. The AER swung close to the Spanish River and here, north of the cemetery, you can still

AER engineers had to locate a pass through the white wall formed by the spectacular Lacloche Mountains.

see the roadbed. In fact, a bush road follows it for a few kilometres east.

The Trans-Canada Highway, Highway 17, skirts along the south edge of Nairn and is your route to McKerrow. (The AER is difficult to follow as it plunges through the bush for the next 15 kilometres.) One of the most attractive stations that the CPR constructed on its Sault branch stood at McKerrow. A storey-and-a-half building, it had dormers tucked into its sweeping chateauesque roof. The Espanola station, a short distance south, was an AER-style building fully two storeys in height, and the last of its kind on the line. The CPR demolished both.

From Highway 17 take Highway 6 south to Espanola; the view of the pulp and paper mill from the bridge that carries you across the Spanish River is stunning. Near the mill you can see the neat stores and streets of the original company townsite. But the town has grown beyond the bounds of the old townsite and is now a sprawling and modern community.

Drive south from Espanola on Highway 6, a twisting road that switchbacks over the white quartzite spine of the Lacloche Mountains, among the province's most spectacular. Here the line remains in use as far as a dock at Little Lacloche Island and passes through communities like Whitefish Falls and the Ojibway town of Birch Island. Wil-

The AER's railway swing bridge at Little Current is still the only land access to Manitoulin island.

lisville, tucked into the craggy peaks, is an interesting company town, with identical houses for the workers who laboured in a mountain quarry. It is east of Highway 6 on Tower Road. Between the Lacloche Island dock and Little Current the line sits abandoned.

To reach the last ghosts on the line continue on Highway 6 to Little Current on Manitoulin Island. On the north side of the channel are the barren fields of what was Turner, the AER's once busy coal yard with cranes, boarding houses, a roundhouse, and water tank. Today it sits vacant. Manitoulin Island is the world's largest freshwater island. And it has no highway bridge to it, so to reach the town of Little Current you must cross on the railway bridge. The swing bridge, planked in for cars, allows only one-way traffic, and in summer opens for ten minutes on the hour to allow the passage of boats through the popular North Channel. Although proposals have been made to replace the structure, it remains a local landmark.

Little Current, the former terminus of the AER, has retained no legacy of its railway heritage other than the bridge. The AER's modest wooden station, the tracks, and other railway buildings have all gone. Nevertheless, it remains a pleasant lakeside community and the gateway to the island itself with its cliffs, its tossing waters, its charming fishing villages, and its resilient native legends and culture. Yet no railway penetrated beyond Little Current.

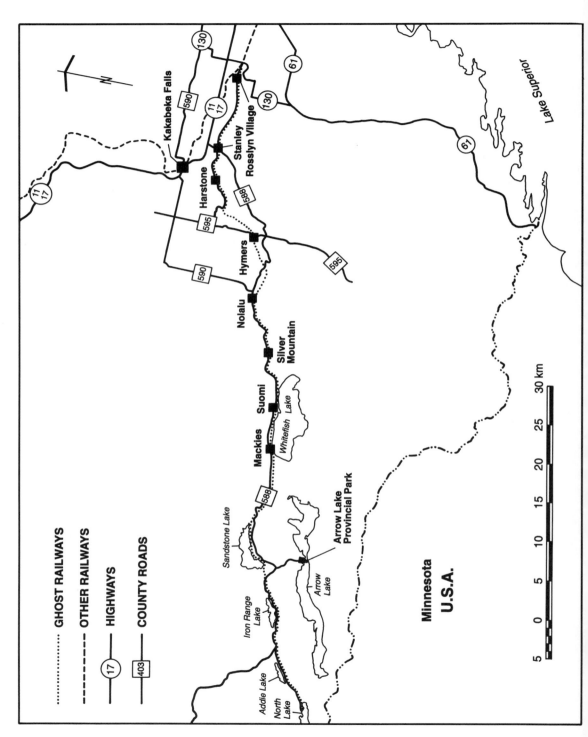

CHAPTER TWENTY-SIX

The Port Arthur Duluth and Western:
The Ghost Railway to Nowhere

Backgrounder

In 1875 the railway age reached the north
shore of Lake Superior. That summer a
steamer crammed with politicians and dignitar-
ies chugged away from Prince Arthur's Landing, then a huddle of log government buildings and outfitters, and docked at the bank of
the Kaministiquia River. Here, near a fur trad-
ing post named Fort William, the elite of this
remote outpost would break ground for the
building of a railway, one that would link the
nation of Canada and become, in the words of
some, our national dream. That railway was
the CPR.

But the good will of that summer degen-
erated into a bitter rivalry when the residents of Prince Arthur's Landing (later Port
Arthur) realized that Fort William would
reap the benefits: the railway yards, the development, and most important of all, the
rise in land values, and that they would
gain none. In desperation they constructed
a private line to cover the seven miles to
the CPR but were refused permission to
link with it. This line, originally called the

Prince Arthur's Landing and Kaministiquia
Railway, was revived in 1883, this time as
the Thunder Bay Colonization Railway,
and this time with more ambitious plans.
The new promoters would build the railway — eighty-six miles long with sixteen
station stops — beyond the CPR and on to
the U.S., where American interests were
proposing a line known as the Alger Smith
Railroad north from Duluth, Minnesota.
The two would link at a remote, forested
Minnesota settlement called Gunflint. A
rich deposit of iron had been discovered
here which would make the railway builders wealthy beyond their dreams.

The Canadians changed the name to
Port Arthur Duluth and Western (PDW),
built their portion to the border, and
waited. But the American portion was
never built. While never officially admitting
it, the exasperated Canadians extended the
line across the border to the mine, and had
the iron to themselves. Along the route
were vast supplies of lumber and silver, and
the prospects for the PDW never looked
better. But these resources all ran out, and

Passengers pose while waiting for the train. (TBM)

by 1900 the line had earned the nickname, "Poverty Agony Distress and Want." Others called it simply the "Pee-Dee."

The line was not without its romantic appeal, becoming the subject of the popular novel, "The Country Beyond" by American author James Oliver Curwood. But there was little romance in the business of running a railway. Had it not been for the ever-present railway builders, MacKenzie and Mann of the Canadian Northern, the PDW might have suffered a quick demise. But the two were looking for an undervalued line that would give their CNo a route into Port Arthur and Fort William, preferably with land along the land. The PDW did just that.

The Canadian Northern was built from Manitoba and linked with the PDW at Stanley Junction, 18 miles west of Fort William. These were the 18 miles that the CNo was after. The remaining 68 miles were of little use to it and received only mixed train service. Then in 1909, a devastating forest fire raced across the Ontario-Minnesota border, destroying the trestle that crossed into the U.S. The railway thereafter ended at North Lake on the Ontario side.

Later, to reduce some of the grade near Stanley, the CNo engineers constructed a cut-off that branched northwesterly from Twin City to Kakabeka Falls, leaving Stanley suddenly on a dead-end line. With less and less business, the line quickly became a money loser. In 1938 the CNR, then the owner of the CNo, abandoned the route west of Twin City and the last train ran on March 24.

All Aboard

Despite the remoteness for most Ontarians, the search for the PDW provides a varied and scenic excursion. Start by following Rosslyn Road west from Highway 61 in Thunder Bay and drive eight kilometres to Twin City. One half kilometre west of Highway 130 the CNR track, which still operates, crosses from south to north to follow the route of the CNo to Rainy River and then to Manitoba. The route of the PDW ran straight west and is still visible at this point. You can follow it by staying on Rosslyn Road to the village of Rosslyn. The little station survived the demise of the railway and was used for storage in 1980s. Two kilometres past Rosslyn the pavement ends ass the road now begins to follow the former right of way. You are now in the engineer's cab for 16 kilometres.

Your next "station," at the intersection of Highway 588, is Stanley. Briefly serving as the important junction between the CNo line from the west and the PDW, Stanley boasted a hotel, coal dock, water tank and a two-storey station with operators on duty around the clock. But when the cut-off was complete, Stanley ceased to be important.

From Stanley, cross the highway and continue west on the right of way. Another two kilometres brings you to the actual site of the junction where the original CNo line swung north on the east bank of the Kaministiquia River, while PDW crossed the river and continued west. Keep travelling west on the PDW route and cross the Kaministiqua River on a surviving railway bridge, now covered with a deck to permit cars. From here the railway was built to follow the banks of Whitefish Creek. The road stays on the right of way for a further six kilometres before swinging away to the north.

Continue on the road as it bends west and comes to Highway 595, which you follow south into Hymers. Here the history of the railway is celebrated with an historical plaque, erected at the site of the station. Much of old Hymers, the railway town, is gone now, replaced by new homes belonging to Thunder Bay commuters. Drive south from the plaque on the highway to come to the Hymers museum housed in a former school. Nearby stands the sleek wooden frame of the historic Catholic church.

If you continue driving south from the museum for 1.5 kilometres you reach High-

way 588, the famous Silver Mountain Highway. Before the railway arrived it was the route to the area's famed silver mines, a bounty which had earned the Lakehead its early title as the "silver gateway." The "highway" led to the mother load at Silver Mountain, and still takes you most of the way there, until it digresses, leaving the high plateau in plain view but tantalizingly out of reach.

About four kilometres west of Hymers, where the highway crosses Whitefish Creek, you cross the right of way near a siding called Sellers. The PDW roadbed follows the south bank of the creek into Nolalu, another railway town, named after the North Land Lumber Company. The track

This remote section of the PDW, near the Minnesota border, is now a cottage access road.

ran right up the tiny main street, which you can see on the south side of the highway at the bottom of the valley.

West of Nolalu the roadbed crosses the creek and at times hugs the highway to the station that served the legendary Silver Mountain. It stands yet on the southwest corner of Highways 588 and 590. Station buffs will recognize the style, for the two-storey building with the familiar pyramid roof is virtually identical to the thousands which the CNo pulled from its pattern book and placed across the country.

A short distance further west, still on Highway 588, the waters of Whitefish Lake come into view and mark the beginning of one of the most scenic former railway routes in Ontario, as the PDW here followed the shores of a string of sparkling lakes. As both the right of way and the highway trace the shoreline, you also enter the settlement of Suomi, the historic heart of the Lakehead area's large and vibrant Finnish community.

About 13 kilometres west of Suomi the highway crosses Sandstone Creek. Once over the bridge look for a dirt road leading to the north. Here again you can get onto the right of way and follow the shore of Sandstone Lake. Past the west end of the lake, the route returns to the highway.

The next lake in the chain is Iron Range Lake where, while you are not on the roadbed, you parallel it closely. Two kilometres past the end of the lake, look again for a dirt trail leading south. Here the right of way wends its last thirty kilometres to the Minnesota border. For the first few kilometres it is drivable by car and takes you along the scenic shore of Addie Lake, an area dominated by sheer cliffs of ancient limestone. As you drive this section look among the trees for another of those familiar pyramid roofs. It will be that of the North Lake station, disassembled in the 1970s and moved here to become a cottage.

The remaining miles are overgrown and difficult to trace, but they do let you appreciate how this route became the ghost railway to nowhere.

Bibliography

Andreae, Chrisptopher, *Railway Heritage study in Toronto.*

Andreae, Christopher, *A Historical Railway Atlas of Southwestern Ontario,* C.A. Andreae, London, 1972,

Beaumont, Ralph, *The Credit Valley Railway,* Boston Mills Press, Boston Mills Ontario, 1974.

Bell, Allan, *A Way to the West,* privately published, Barrie, 1991. (The Ottawa Arnprior and Parry Sound Railway)

Bennett, Carol, and D.W. McCuaig, *In Search of the K and P.,* Renfrew Advance, Renfrew Ontario, 1981.

Bohi, Charles W., and Leslie S. Kozma, *Canadian Pacific's Western Depots,* South Platte Press, David City Nebraska, 1993.

Bond, Courtney C.J., *City on the Ottawa, A detailed historical guide to Ottawa,* Queens Printer, Ottawa, 1961.

Bowers, Peter, *Two Divisions to Bluewater,* Boston Mills Press, Erin, 1983, (The Wellington Grey and Bruce)

Bowering Ian, "All Aboard the New York Central, Next station, Cornwall", *Cornwall Standard-Freeholder,* March 28, 1992.

Brault, Dr. Lucien, *The Mile of History,* National Capital Commission, 1981,

Brown, Ron, *50 Unusual Things to see in Ontario,* Boston Mills Press, Erin Ontario, 1989

Brown, Ron, *50 Even More Unusual Things to see In Ontario,* Boston Mills Press, Erin Ontario, 1993,

Brown, Ron, *Ghost Towns of Ontario: A Field Guide,* Polar Bear Press, 1997;

Brown, Ron, *The Train Doesn't Stop Here Any More,* Broadview Press, Peterborough Ontario, 1991,

Canadian Station News, various issues, 1991-1994, Dave Savage, Cobourg Ontario.

Coo, Bill, *Scenic Rail Guide to Central and Atlantic Canada,* Geery de Pencier Books, Toronto, 1983,

Cook, John and Jo Anne, *A Compendium of Southern Ontario Rail Lines 1850-1984,* Rideau Graphics, 1985

Cooper, Charles, *Narrow Gauge for Us,* Boston Mills Press, Erin, 1982. (The Toronto and Nipissing Railway)

Cooper Charles, *Rails to the Lakes,* Boston Mills Press, Erin, 1980. (The Hamilton and Northwestern Railway)

Cornwall Freeholder Souvenir, *New York and Ottawa Railway,* 1901

Cote, Jean-G., "Stean Hauled Silk Trains", *Canadian Rail,* 293, Nov/Dec, 1974.

Currie A.W., *The Grand Trunk Railway of Canada,* University of Toronto Press, 1957.

Dalibard, Jacques, "Getting on the Right Track", *Canadian Heritage,* Vol 10, 1984.

Davis, Jo, ed., *Not a Sentimental Journey, What's Behind the Via Rail Cuts,* Gunbyfield Publishers, 1990,

Denhez, Marc, *"Railway Blues, Stations are Coming Down in a Legal Vacuum"*, Canadian Heritage, #41, 1983.

Denhez, Marc, *Heritage Fights Back,* Fitzhenry and Whiteside, Toronto 1978.

Easton, Mel, *"Mel Easton's History of the K and P"*, Perth Courier, 1978,

Edmonson, H.A. and R.V. Francaviglia, *Railroad Station Planbook,* Kalmbach Books, Milwaukee, 1977.

Ferguson, Ted, *Sentimental Journey, An oral History of Train Travel,* Doubleday, Canada Ltd, Toronto, 1985.

Folkins, Wentworth, and Michael Bradley, *The Great Days of Canadian Steam, A Wentworth Folkins Portfolio,* Hounslow Press, Willowdale Ontario, 1988,

Garland, Aileen, *"Gardens Along the Right of Way"*, Manitoba Pageant, Winter 1977.

Geddes, Hilda, *The Canadian Mississippi River,* Snow Road Ontario, 1988.

Grant, H.R., and Charles Bohi, *The Country Railroad Station in America,* Centre for Western Studies, Sioux Falls, North Dakota, 1988.

Heels, Charles, *Railroad Recollections,* Alan R. Capon ed, Museum Restoration Service, Bloomfield Ontario, 1980.

Illustrated Historical Atlases of various Ontario counties, 1870s - 1890s., H. Beldon company, Toronto.

Jackson, John, and John Burtniak, *Railways in the Niagara Peninsula,* Mika Publishing, Belleville, 2978.

Kalman Harold, *Railway Hotels and the Development of the Chateau Style in Canada,* University of Victoria, Maltwood Studies in Architectural History, Volume 1, 1968,

Kalman, Harold, *"What to do with all those Redundant Stations"*, Canadian Heritage, December, 1980.

Lebrecht, Sue, "Rails to Trails Concept Growing", *The Saturday Star,* September 21, 1991.

Legget, Robert F., *Railways of Canada*, Douglas and McIntyre, VAncouver, 1973,

Liddell, K., *I'll Take the Train,* Western Producer Prairie Books, Saskatoon, 1977,

MacKay, Niall, *Over the Hills to Georgian Bay, Picture History of the Ottawa Arnprior and Parry Sound Railway,* Boston Mills Press, Erin Ontario, 1081.

McDougall, Terry, *"How We Won the Battle of the Railway Stations"*, Canadian Heritage magazine, Winter, 1988,

Marin, Clive and Frances, *Stormont Dundas and Glengarry, 1945-1978,* Mika Publishing, 1982

Mika, Nick and Helma, with Donald M. Wilson, *Illustrated History of Canadian Railways,* Mika Publishing, Belleville, 1986,

National Liberal Caucus, *Report of the Federal Liberal Task Force on Via Rail,* November 1989.

Newell, Dianne, and Ralph Greenhill, *Survivals, Aspects of Industrial Archaeology in Ontario,* Boston Mills Press, Erin Ontario, 1989,

Ontario Dept of Public Records and Archives, "The Port Arthur, Duluth and Western Railway Company," *Historical Plaque Press Release,* Sept, 1970.

Ontario Heritage Foundation, *A Railway Station Information Kit, An Aid for the Conservation of Heritage Railway Stations,* Toronto, nd

Ontario Heritage Foundation, *Planning for Heritage Railway Stations,* in cooperation with Canadian National Railways, and VIA Rail, 2 volumes, Toronto, 1987,

Ontario Heritage Foundation, *A Study of Canadian Pacific*'s Heritage Railway Properties, in cooperation with CP Rail and VIA Rail, Toronto,1989,

Whitby This Week, *"Historic Train Station May be Saved"*, Mar 16, 1988.

Pennington, Myles, *Railways and Other Ways,* Williamson and Company, Toronto, 1894.

Public Archives of Canada, RG 30 M ACC 78903/42, *Grand Trunk Railway station plans,*

Public Archives of Canada, RG 46, Series C-11-1,, Volume 1415, File 11389.1, 1945, *Station Plans,*

Pubic Archives of Canada, RG 46, Series C-11-1, Vol 1448, File 17061, Closings of Stations on Weekends and Holidays, 1911-1961,

Public Archives of Canada, RG 46, Series C-11-1, Vol 1538, File 18540.25, *Naming Railway Stations,* part 1, 1916-1929; Part 2, 1931-1952,

Public Archives of Canada, RG 46, Series C-11-1, Vol 1526, File 10729, *CP Standard Plans for Western Lines, 1929,*

Public Archives of Canada, RG 12, Vol 1345, File 3350-3 *History of Government Control and regulation of railways in Canada, 1891-1953,*

Rempel, J.I., *The Town of Leaside, A Brief History,* East York Historical Society, Toronto, 1982.

Richards J., and John M MacKenzie, *The Railway Station, a Social History,* Oxford University Press, 1986

Robinson, Dean, *Railway Stratford,* Boston Mills Press, Erin Ontario, 1989

Stamp Robert M., *Riding the Radials,* Boston Mills Press, Erin, 1989,

Stevens, G.R., *Canadian National Railways,* 2 Vol, Clarke Irwin and Co., Toronto., 1962.

Talman J. J., *"Impact of the railway on a Pioneer Community",* Canadian Historical Association, Ottawa, 1955.

Tennant, Robert D. *Canada Southern Country,* Boston Mills Press, Erin ontario, 1991.

Thompson, Allan, *"Summerhill station slated for yet another lease on life",* Toronto Star, May 29, 1990.

Todd, John, "Poverty, Agony, Distress and Want! The PAD&W Railway", *Canadian Rail Magazine,* St. Constant Quebec, 1974.

The Toronto Sunday World, "Memories of a Monumental Mistake" (The Toronto Belt Line Railway), Toronto November 11, 1923.

Town of Orangeville BIA, *CPR Station Redevelopment,* R.J. Long Consultants, Ltd., 1984.

Tozer, Ron and Dan Strickland, *A Pictorial History of Algonquin Park,* The Friends of Algonquin Park and the Ontario Ministry of Natural Resources, 1986,

Trout, J.M. and Edward, *The Railways of Canada for 1871,* Monetary Times, Toronto 1871, Reprinted, Coles Publishing Company, Toronto 1970.

Walker, Dr Frank N., *Four Whistles to Wood Up,* Upper Canada Railway Society, Toronto, 1953.

Von Baeyer, E., *Rhetoric and Roses, a History of Canadian Gardening,* Fitzhenry and Whiteside, Markham, 1984,

Wilkins Taylor, *Haliburton by Rail and the I.B.& O.* privately published, Lindsay Ontario, 1992.

Wilmot Elizabeth, *Faces and Places Along the Railway,* Gage Publishing, Toronto 1979.

Wilmot Elizabeth, *Meet Me at the Station,* Gage Publishing, Toronto, 1976.

Wilmot Elizabeth, *When Any Time Was Train Time,* Boston Mills Press, Erin Ontario, 1992.

Wilson Dale, *Algoma Eastern Railway,* Nickel Belt Rails, #1, Sudbury, 1977

Wilson Donald M., *Lost Horizons,* Mika Publishing, Belleville Ontario, 1986,

Wilson, Donald M., *Ontario and Quebec Railway,* Mika Publishing, Belleville, 1984,

Index

Photograph Credits

OA: Ontario Archives
PA: Public Archives of Canada
UCM: United Counties Museum, Cornwall
APM: Algonquin Museum
LA: Len Appleyard collection
DS: Dave Spaulding collection
TBM: Thunder Bay Museum
MTL: Metro Toronto Library
LCM: Lennox and Addington County Museum

All other photographs are from the author's collection